GOLD IS REAL MONEY

HOW WE THE PEOPLE ARE AT WAR AGAINST BIG BANKS AND BIG GOVERNMENT

I0467713

Legal Disclaimer

Although the author and publisher have made every effort to ensure that the information in this book was correct at press time, the author and publisher do not assume and hereby disclaim any liability to any party for any loss, damage, or disruption caused by errors or omissions, whether such errors or omissions result from negligence, accident, or any other cause. Statements of facts are not guaranteed in any way.

The opinions presented are the opinions of the author alone. Do not make any investment decisions based upon any opinions presented in this book. This book is not investment advice. Seek out a qualified financial advisor to guide you through the complexities of investments.

Acknowledgements

First, I want to thank my wife Laura. Writing this book has been a journey. As they say, the journey sometimes is just as important, if not more important, than the destination. This book took a long time to write. It took even longer to research. Then to edit and rewrite. Then rewrite again. The book was a long time coming. The number of hours involved were staggering. I feel very blessed to have a wife like Laura. Not every wife would tolerate their husband committing so much time and effort into a project such as this. There were many late nights, early mornings, and weekend hours devoted to undertaking this massive project. My wife did a lot more than tolerate...she endorsed it and encouraged me to follow my passion. She is a rare breed. I love you sweetie.

I want to thank my parents, my aunt, and grandmother for all the support over my lifetime. You instilled a work ethic in me that gave me the discipline to tackle a challenge such as writing this book. Thank you for all your love and encouragement.

I want to thank my dad for being there for me. You acted as a sounding board for my concepts and ideas for this book. You helped immensely by reading and then re-reading my many versions and drafts of this book. You are the smartest and most insightful person I know. You have a calm demeanor. You have truly been a role model for me. I'm happy to have you not only as my dad, but as my best friend as well. I can never repay you.

I want to thank all the people who have helped me along the way by contributing to my knowledge base on the subjects in this book. There are simply too many people to list individuals by name. They have come from all areas and walks of life. There were economists, bullion dealers, small business owners, large business owners, corporate executives, coin collectors, lawyers, military officers, and laymen of every stripe. These individuals may appear very different, but they all share one common trait: they graciously gave of their time. They answered my questions as I picked their brain for more knowledge. They were generous with their time. I will be forever grateful to these individuals.

I underestimated how much time a book such as this takes to bring to fruition. Even so, I really enjoyed doing the research involved. It helped that I have a passion for the subject matter. I am a proud American and love this country. I believe in the Constitution and the liberties it bestows on us. The United States is the best nation on earth. We The People have a personal responsibility to defend our country from all enemies, foreign and domestic. I hope the reader will find the pages of this book eye opening. God Bless America!

Table of Contents

Introduction

What is it about this yellow colored metal that makes people lust after it so much? Since the beginning of civilization people have fought for it, waged war because of it, hoarded it, used it in trade, and displayed it to decorate themselves. In the history of the world, it has no equal. Nothing has come evenly remotely close to its stature.

Sure, a diamond may be "a girl's best friend" when speaking of engagement rings, but chances are that diamond stone will be set on a gold ring. This is hardly a new trend. Kings have been using their crowns made of gold to symbolize their wealth, power, and prestige since antiquity. De Beer's ad agency convinced almost all men in America to give up three months pay on average to buy those engagement rings, but this has only been since the early 20th century. Gold has roots that go back far deeper. It was treasured in ancient times just as it is now.

Geologically speaking, gold is unrivaled as well. It is rare and durable. One of only 2 metals whose natural color is not gray/silver in tone (the other being copper). Copper oxidizes by reacting with oxygen to turn a green patina on the outside. Not so for gold. Gold does not react or tarnish or oxidize. This is why gold is said to be "Noble". It is more noble than copper, more noble than silver which tarnishes. As far as rarity goes diamonds are nonsense. They are pretty and extremely durable but they are made of carbon – one of the most common of earth's elements. Gold is extremely rare.

Because of its rarity and universal appeal, gold has been used as money for thousands of years. From ancient Greece and Rome to the United States in the not so distant past. It is only recently that the governments around the world have not only abandoned gold but have actually tried all sorts of means to discourage the use of. Time may well show this to be a worldwide experiment in the decoupling of gold with national currencies to be a very dangerous period in history.

The United States of America *had* one of the best (if not THE best) monetary systems in the world. As the United States emerged as a new nation after defeating the British Empire in the Revolutionary War, our young country was essentially broke. During the revolutionary war, a paper money system using "continental currency" had been used and this followed the war out of necessity. This system did not end well. This is why our founding fathers set about to create a stable and honest money system – the failure of the continental was still painfully in their minds as they were the ones who lived through this mess. After over 200 years the phrase "not worth a continental" is still in our lexicon to refer to this first system. The founding fathers based the monetary system on gold and silver. The first U.S. gold coins were minted back in 1795. This system had an incredible run, as the nation rose to become a superpower in the world.

Behind the scenes, things weren't always going well for our monetary system. Silver stayed in use up to 1964 and some form of a gold standard lasted until 1971 (or more accurately until 1933 for individual U.S. Citizens).

Why the change? What happened to derail such a solid system of honest money based on gold as its backbone? Why would our country turn its back on a monetary system that enabled it to power to preeminent status? There were a couple of instances when our nation was really going through major issues such as Civil War, Panics, The Great Depression. Unfortunately, there were sneaky interest groups who used these very tough challenges that our nation faced to advance their own agendas. They often pretended that they were trying to help. In reality, they were really only trying to help their own causes.

There is a theme that runs through this book showing how the powerful banking interests used the calamities our country faced to further their secret agendas. During the Civil War, banks tried to take advantage by offering loans at usurious interest rates. This was mild compared to what was coming. In the early 20th Century, the bankers devised a plan to literally take over the U.S. money supply. By this time, they were not content to just charging high interest like before. This time, they wanted to actually be the ones printing the money and deciding on interest rates. They just needed an excuse. The panic of 1907 gave them that excuse to carry out their plans. The Federal Reserve System was a conspiracy from the very beginning. The idea was to privatize control of the money supply in the United States. They got their wish in 1913 when the Federal Reserve System was created by duping, threatening, and bribing Congress and the Public at large. Despite it's name, the Federal Reserve is NOT a part of the U.S. government. It is a private Central Bank owned by some of the largest for-profit banking concerns in the world. Twenty years later, in 1933 "The Fed" as it's commonly referred to, went a step further by convincing President Roosevelt that severing the dollar from gold for the American people was the way to go. Years later, they managed to have it severed completely in 1971.

This is how we arrive at our present condition. The Fed is owned by a private banking cartel. Since money no longer needs to be backed by gold, the Fed can create money out of thin air. It does this for the benefit of its for-profit owners without any regard for the good of the nation or for the American people. It operates to fulfill its own purposes with impunity, and all the while, it has no accountability to anyone. The Fed and the U.S. government have this cozy, and unholy relationship. Together, the Fed enables the government to get bigger and bigger. What happens as a result? We have a government that can run amok. We get military adventurism, which leads to the military industrial complex growing in size and power. We get massively expensive programs like Obamacare. We get a bloated bureaucracy with multiple layers of government. We get all kinds of taxes levied on us. The government becomes big and inefficient and relies on the Fed for their big bloated survival. The privately owned banking cartel that owns the Fed ensures its own existence will be maintained. None of this is good for the American people. We The People get a big, bloated government that interferes with our lives. We get a central bank in the Fed that is accountable to nobody. In other words, We The People get screwed.

The elected officials of the United States let this go on because they are beholden to these bankers, which frequently finance their political campaigns. The United States government itself has become addicted to all the easy cash and credit the Fed provides for them. The ones who lose are the American people. The dollar, which was backed by gold and silver, is now no more than pieces of paper. We, the American people, now conduct all of our transactions, investing, and saving with this Monopoly money that consistently loses value all the time. The large banks hold the real money – they hold the physical gold. This, while the Fed and other central banks of the world tell us that gold is not relevant anymore. The truth is, the big banks and the government hate gold when it is in the hands of the public. They secretly love gold, when it is in their hands. This period may well go down in history as the best hat trick the bankers have ever been able to pull off. The problem is, the trick is on us.

There should be outrage over moving so far so fast to a system that is basically a government endorsed Ponzi scheme of paper money which is backed by nothing. But this took place not all at once, but in a series of steps. This book will chronicle the major events that little by little chipped away at our nation's sound money system. This reminds us of the story of a frog being boiled alive. If a frog is placed in a pot of boiling water, the frog will jump out because of the pain. But if a frog is placed in a pot with room temperature water that is slowly heated, it will stay put, not realizing the danger and will be slowly cooked to death. This metaphor describes the situation Americans are facing. If the money was suddenly and completely taken off the gold standard long ago, people would not have tolerated it. You would have had open rebellion in the streets. But the destruction of our money took place in increments, to trick people into thinking everything was OK. This is not just the United States. The whole world has moved to a system not backed by gold or anything else of tangible value.

The dollar as we know it is a fiction. It was presented as the great salvation for our capitalist system to survive and thrive during difficult times. It has only

10

caused the population to incur a devastating reduction of wealth. The almighty dollar is a false prophet. It promises to create wealth and prosperity for all with its easy money policies. It gets its strength by offering government and the people something for nothing. People become deluded into believing the idea that you can create all this wealth by simply printing more of the dollars. It sounds like a great trick. It even seems to work in the very short term, which gives credence and legitimacy to the paper promises that the dollar offers. All of this makes people accepting of the paper dollar. It lures them in. But this path doesn't lead to some utopian heaven. It is *not* a salvation for hard economic times.

Choosing paper money is the road to perdition instead. It leads to unstable money. It leads to enormous debt accumulation. It leads to unnecessary war by enabling governments to fund military adventurism. It leads to inflation, which is nothing more than a continual loss of value of a currency. Inflation is a secret tax on people – the hard work of people is stolen by the currency constantly weakening. This especially hurts the poor and middle class. Given a long enough time frame, the survival rate of all paper currency is ultimately zero.

The blame for all of this ultimately rests at the feet of the big international banking cartels. They got their way not all at once, but in increments throughout history. The people being forced to fight powerful bankers is not a new thing. Jesus himself fought this fight. "And Jesus went into the temple of God, and cast out all them that sold and bought in the temple, and overthrew the tables of the moneychangers, and the seats of them that sold doves"(Mathew 21:12)(1). "And said unto them, it is written, My house shall be called the house of prayer; but ye have made it a den of thieves!"(Mathew 21:13)(1). The moneychangers were the bankers of the time. I think it's pretty clear how Jesus felt about the bankers based on his own words – he called them thieves, as well as his actions – he didn't just tell them to leave, he physically overturned their tables. Fast forward some 2,000 years later, and We The People are still fighting the greedy bankers.

This is not a fight the people started. This fight was brought on by the large banking cartels. They are the ones who made war against our sound money and ultimately, against our liberty. This puts us all in a situation where We The People are at war against the big banks and the big, bloated government that has resulted. This is not a war fought with bullets or tanks, but rather by winning over hearts and minds. The big banks have done a great job of convincing most people that the Federal Reserve is somehow a part of the government. But in this modern age, it is harder and harder for them to keep up this façade. Information now moves too fast and freely for them to continuously rely on disinformation to cement their power. It is harder to keep duping people. This is a good thing, because if we all do not wake up to what is going on, these big banks will end up destroying our country.

What can we do about this? We would all be wise to remember that during the period of 1795 to 1933/1971 (whichever year you choose to pick) The United States had the best growth and strongest run of maybe any nation in the history of the world. Gold was not simply incidental in all of this. It was what backed the entire financial system and enabled the American Miracle to happen . (There were a couple of major exceptions (American Civil War and the 1933 gold confiscation) which we will go into further in the chapters ahead).

Societies that move away from solid asset backed money eventually crumble and fail, usually in dramatic fashion. I am sure that every one of them felt that "this time it's different". It wasn't. Is this what awaits the United States and the world? Or is it "different this time"? Is our age really so special to be able to avoid the disasters that befell on all other civilizations that decided gold was no longer relevant and ended up paying the ultimate price for their hubris? Read on and you be the judge...

Chapter 1 - Benefits of using gold as money

Gold has inherent properties that lend it certain advantages. It has these traits that make it ideal for use as money.

Rarity

Gold is rare. It's really rare. This fact alone is a property you want in sound money. Everyone dreams of money growing on trees. It's such a cliché to say or read "money doesn't grow on trees". What if our ancestors had decided that for money, tree leaves would be a good fit? Wouldn't that make all our wildest dreams come true? Well, no, actually, it wouldn't. The reason is simple – there would be a supply issue right off the bat. As in too much supply. Trees are abundant and leaves are even more abundant. We know this to be true in New England when it's time to do the spring and fall cleanups. Those trees dump their leaves all over the place. Leaves are so common that not only do they *not* have value, they actually have a *negative value* to us. They cost either our time and labor to deal with, or else cost us money to hire people to get rid of them.

Gold doesn't grow on trees. It has to be mined. Go out into your backyard and start digging. Do you think you'll find any gold anytime soon? In most of the U.S., you simply won't – none exists. So no matter how much you dig, you just won't find any. Some parts of the country do have gold deposits. I have an aunt that went on a trip to

Alaska a couple of years ago. She told me that she went on a gold panning excursion. The tour company brought her and others to a river where they literally panned for gold, like you see portrayed in all those old movies. The idea is simple enough. For the areas that have gold deposits, the river water can bring small amounts of gold downstream that can be shifted on a pan for people to find. I've always been amazed at this. I think if my property or town had such a place, I could take up gold prospecting as a new hobby! In my aunt's case, she got really into it, and worked the pan for all it was worth for a couple hours. And low and behold, she found gold! Once you get over the coolness factor, the result that she showed me was not very impressive, to say the least. A few specks of gold the size of grains of sand. If you just happen to live in such an area, it could be a hobby you take up for exercise, with a nice side effect of getting a tiny amount of gold as your exercise reward. But I share this story because I think it does an excellent job illustrating just how rare gold really is, even in areas that are known to have gold deposits.

Even when gold is found in what we consider deposits, or gold mines, it is not an easy task to obtain it. Gold mines exist, but often are far underground, which can be a mile or two. It's hot, dangerous work to bring up the gold. And understand what they are bringing up...it's not what you and I think of as "gold". It is gold ore. The element gold is trapped in rock. When you see photos of stuff coming out of the mines, it looks like a bunch of rock. The mining companies then have to go through a whole refining process where they crush the ore apart and use chemicals to get the gold out. You don't just find nice big hunks of pure gold. Refining gold from this ore is a tough, time consuming, energy intensive process.

For money to have value, it can't just grow on trees. It has to be something that is hard to get. Otherwise, the money will just lose its value and become worth nothing. This has happened to un-backed, paper currencies of the world in the past. The money became worth about as much as paper, which is basically zero. Gold fits the rarity test perfectly.

Durable

Gold is durable. It's a metal. You wouldn't want to use something delicate as money. Using fancy glass sculptures wouldn't work out so well. Just imagine if you dropped it...goodbye weekly pay just like that. Ideally, you want a material that can stand the test of time.

Gold coins from ancient times are still with us, in one form or another. They either survived in their original coin state, or were melted down to make new gold coins or jewelry. In fact, what we hold in our hands today as necklaces, coins, wedding rings, or whatever...the gold in that item is not necessarily new from the mine. Chances are good that at least a portion of the gold contained in that gold item is generations old...scrap that was recycled many times over.

Gold's durability is almost unmatched. Even though it has the benefit of being metal, it does not suffer from other metal's weaknesses. It does not rust, oxidize, or corrode. It is one of the most inert substances, which means it does not react to many things. If you find an old treasure ship sunken hundreds of years ago, you can be sure that the gold coins will be there. It doesn't matter if it's in fresh water or salt water. These harsh conditions will ultimately destroy a wooden ship and great ships made of iron given a long enough time frame. Yet the gold will not so much as tarnish, let alone be destroyed.

You need durability in money. You wouldn't want to work and save your whole life only to find that the money you're using has rotted, corroded, rusted, etc. Gold money is sound money physically and theoretically.

Fungible

Gold is "fungible" which means that all gold is the same and interchangeable. This does not mean that all gold coins, jewelry, bars, etc have the same *amount* of gold. There are differences in gold purity in these items, and there are a number of ways to express this such as Karats, %, fineness. But as gold is an element, fungible means gold is gold. There is no such thing as good gold or better gold, bad gold, etc. gold is just gold. and all gold is the same. Again, don't be confused – the metrics of purity only tell us ways to measure how much actual gold is present in a particular item. Once that is figured out, the gold itself is all the same. This is important because gold has a great edge over other commodities that are not fungible. A great example of a commodity that is not fungible is a diamond. If diamonds were being used as money, you would have very, very complicated transactions. Diamonds are not at all the same. Their value depends on such metrics as color, clarity, cut, size, whether inclusions are present, etc. using them in trade would be a nightmare because they are all different and unique. Gold has a definite advantage, as once you determine the gold content of an item, trade can take place on a price per gold basis. It doesn't matter where it was mined in the world. Gold is gold.

Divisible

Related to the idea of being fungible. Since all gold is the same, this property serves to make gold divisible. Meaning if you had a bar of gold and wanted to pay someone in gold, you could cut off half or a quarter of the gold bar to pay them. (NOTE: *never* do this! People want their bars and coins in good condition, not cut up!). This is more of a thought exercise of what could be done. In the real world, people don't cut up bars or coins or anything else. But what is done is giving change. If I have to pay you 5 ounces of gold for an item I want to buy, and I give you a 10 ounce bar, then you give me change with either a 5 ounce bar or 5 one ounce bars. In real life, people didn't exchange bars. This is just for illustration of the property of gold. What people *did* do years ago was the use of gold coins. If something was for sale for $15 dollars and I had a $20 gold coin that I pay you, then you would give me back a $5 gold coin as my change. The fact that gold is all the same makes divisibility and (in the real world) change possible.

Hard to Counterfeit

Gold is very difficult to counterfeit. This is especially true of gold coins because you can look up what the size and weight of the coin in question should be. People who are new to gold coins often wonder why a dishonest person or company can't just make a coin out of steel and then gold plate the coin to make it look authentic. The answer is that they can. And every once in a while, they do. The counterfeiter can make a coin in just the right proportions: the right diameter, with the right thickness. If a counterfeiter does this, the coin will *look* perfectly authentic. But if you're at all familiar with that gold coin, as soon as you pick it up, you will notice the coin is a lot lighter than what it should be. If you're not familiar with the coin, then you can weigh it and it will be a lot lighter than it should be. A counterfeiter can make a coin with the correct weight, but then will either have to make the coin diameter larger or the thickness much thicker to add the extra weight. In this case, the coin will weigh correctly, but the size and/or thickness will be off to add the extra weight. Because gold has such a density, and is so heavy a metal, there really isn't a good way for counterfeiters to fake it. Something has to give when using base metals to compensate for the weight difference. Counterfeiters could use a metal like platinum which is even heavier than gold and then gold plate it. That might be passable. But platinum is hard to work with and is usually more expensive than gold, so this would be a no go for the counterfeiter. The metal tungsten has been in the news lately. Tungsten has a weight similar to gold and it was used in a few very large bars of gold. The counterfeiters had taken a genuine gold bar, drilled holes in it, and filled those holes with tungsten. For their trouble, they got to keep the gold they drilled out of the bar. The element tungsten is extremely hard to work with, and there is no evidence of tungsten gold coins, at least not to any great degree. It comes down to buying from reputable dealers. A lot of the fake gold coins are actually still made out of gold. Counterfeiters use real gold to try to fake a rare coin – rare date, rare mintmark. Or use real gold of just a slightly lower purity, but real gold nonetheless.

I suppose anything of value can, and does, get counterfeited. It is probably a lot easier to counterfeit and pass fake paper money than gold money. None of the weight and material aspects of counterfeiting gold need to be overcome. A home scanner and printer have come so far in the last decade. The fact that the U.S. has changed the design of our paper money to try and thwart counterfeiters is an admission by our government that there is indeed a problem. From time to time, you hear about what is called a "Supernote", a counterfeit note that is done so well, that it is virtually indistinguishable from the real thing. The government tries to keep it quiet, because they need people to have faith in the dollar, both in the theory of it, and in the physical form. Since confidence is the only thing that gives our un-backed paper money any value at all, the government has a great incentive to keep things as quiet as possible.

High Value Per Weight

Gold is very valuable. Because of its high value, you don't need huge amounts of it to have large purchasing power. Compare this to copper, which is valuable, but not really a "precious" metal. Think about an economy where all we had to pay for items were copper coins. If the coins got successively larger by the denomination, then we would need some very big copper coins. In fact, we would all need to be bodybuilders, because these giant copper coins would resemble weights. That would be so impractical in commerce. Wood has some value – for firewood, building materials, lumber. If wood was used as money, we would all need 18 wheelers to lug around vast amounts of the stuff, and need warehouses to store it all. Very impractical. Owing to its rarity and desirability, gold has the high value density that makes it very convenient. We can fit a vast amount of purchasing power right in our pockets with gold.

Desirable

Gold is desirable, in and of itself. No government or ruler had to force gold upon the people. It was the people themselves that decided that gold has value. People concurred long ago that because of all these properties mentioned in this chapter, gold was special. People chose gold as their preference to decorate themselves with jewelry. People hoard it. Why? People want it. It has a look and feel that people find pleasing. Paper money totally lacks this – when was the last time you saw someone wearing dollar bills around their neck or wrists?

People chose gold over the centuries. A great example can be found in the bible. The Three Wise Men (also known as the Magi) visited a baby Jesus bearing gifts. What were those gifts? "...gold, frankincense and myrrh that the magi presented to Jesus, according to the Gospel of Matthew (2:11). These valuable items were standard gifts to honor a king or deity in the ancient world: gold as a precious metal, frankincense as perfume or incense, and myrrh as anointing oil."(1)

When people hear these gifts, most people only have a hazy guess at what Frankincense and Myrrh are. All three of these gifts were obviously very valuable back in the ancient world, as they were gifts fit for a king or a god. You wouldn't insult them by bringing cheap stuff. These gifts were precious indeed. Frankincense and myrrh have long since lost their relevance. They still technically "exist", but when was the last time you heard of someone giving or receiving them as gifts? I would guess never. Compare the obscurity of these two gifts with gold. When we hear this story, gold is the only one that seems to fit, because we can all relate to it. It's one thing to look up these other items and find out that they were valuable once; it's quite another to know from our own personal lives the value placed on gold. When you stop and think about it long enough, it's really amazing...something that was prized 2,000 years ago is also prized to this very day. The other two gifts actually make more sense in terms of our expectations. When you consider how different life was in ancient times to the life we are living today in the modern world, you would expect that all three gifts would be obsolete now.

I think it speaks a tremendous amount about gold being universally desirable. It was highly valued then just as it is now. In addition to desirability, it also speaks to gold's durability, a trait we previously mentioned. But in addition to physical durability, gold has a durability of desire. People want it now just as they did thousands of years ago. It certainly looks different than other elements. Gold is one of only two metals whose natural color is not silver/gray in color. So, needless to say, it has a unique look going in its favor.

No Counter Party Risk

What this means is that gold is a pure asset. All by itself, it is worth something. All paper assets give you a claim of some kind against someone or something else. Another person or institution whether a government or company, or whatever, has to make good on something in order for that piece of paper to be worth anything. This is why when governments fail, the currency and bonds then become worthless. When a company fails, its stock and bonds become worthless. Gold doesn't have this problem. In fact, there are many examples of governments and rulers that minted gold coins and who did not survive after some point in history. Those gold coins continue to be worth their weight in gold...literally.

The specific qualities make for good, sound money. Gold meets all of these criteria. Other contenders had their shot at being money, and were tried in history. These other contenders passed some of the traits discussed here, but failed others. Nothing else can really hold their own against gold. People say "cash is king". Well, *gold* is the undisputed king.

Chapter 2 - Gold Geology

Gold is from out of this world. Really – all the gold ever mined on earth is thought to come from outer space. Huh? How can this be? The BBC News Magazine stated "The idea that gold came from outer space sounds like science fiction, but it has become well-established - it's pretty much received opinion in the field of earth sciences."(1) Basically the idea is this – when the earth was forming billions of years ago, the earth would have been endowed with some gold. The earth at that time was liquid –like lava flowing on the surface. As gold is an extremely heavy metal, it would stand to reason that the gold present would have sunk toward the core. The gold we have on the surface and just below that are mined now is what came from meteors which brought gold and other elements from outer space. Not every scientist believes this, but enough do to make this a prevailing theory.

A common question that comes up is how much gold has been mined so far? In other words, how much gold exists which has been brought up out of the ground at this point? "At the end of 2014, there were 183,600 tonnes of stocks in existence above ground. If every single ounce of this gold were placed Next to each other, the resulting cube of pure gold would only measure 21 metres in any direction. While its rarity endures, the sources of gold have become as geographically-diverse as gold demand.

China is the largest producer in the world in 2014, Accounting for around 15 per cent of total production. Asia as a whole produces 22 per cent of the total newly-mined gold. Central and South America produces around 17 per cent of the total, with North America supplying around 15 per cent.

Around 20 per cent of production comes from Africa and 14 per cent from the CIS region, where new discoveries and new operations offer opportunities for economic growth and development. Recycling Accounts for around one third of the total supply of gold."(2)

Peak Gold?

A discussion of gold supply addresses not only on what has already been mined, but also the question of how much gold is left in the ground? This brings us to the idea of peak gold. Peak gold theory holds that the production of gold from mines will increase until the point is reached that you hit "peak" – the highest rate you can extract gold, and then after peak the production figures begin an irreversible decline in production rate.

The notion of "peak" comes from the oil industry. Back in the 1950's a Shell Oil Company geologist named M. King Hubbert came up with a theory. He studied the production rates of oil wells in the United States and predicted that the rate of production would continuously increase year after year, but that this trend could not endure to infinity. The supply of oil in the ground is fixed and is non-renewable so at some point you will hit a maximum production rate: the Peak. He could see this happen with individual oil fields: They would be discovered, a small amount of oil would be extracted at the beginning until more pump jacks and equipment were brought in, and then the oil would flow and increase year after year. Eventually, the oil production rate would hit a maximum – the peak rate, then as the natural pressure from the well declined, so would the rate of oil recovery. A key to this is that once your past peak, the decline is irreversible. Oil companies would pump in water, natural gas, etc in an effort to drive up the pressure of the well, but this can only do so much – it can help elongate the production curve when plotted on a chart, but not change the overall outcome. Eventually the oil well would be shut down. There would still be oil in the well, but it would no longer be economic to extract it. This is a second key here to his theory – it's not that you run out of oil, but rather you run out of economic oil (cheap oil). On top of this, you don't know you hit peak until after it has passed and you are witnessing the decline phase.

Mr. Hubbert took what he knew about an individual oil well's life cycle and applied this mathematically to the entire U.S. oil industry. He presented his theory to the world in 1956 and predicted that the United States as a nation would hit peak oil between 1965 (worst case scenario) and 1970 (best case scenario). For his efforts, Mr. Hubbert was not rewarded at the time – he was ridiculed by his peers and the media as some kind of doom and gloom quack. As the years passed by, the U.S. Oil industry ended up producing the most oil in 1970, and after this year, began to decline year after year. (this decline was only partially halted by Alaskan oil coming online in 1977 and ramping up in the mid 1980's. The current technique of fracking has allowed U.S. production of oil to shoot up in the short term. The jury is still out on whether this will be able/ allowed by environmental concerns to contine). So in the end, Mr Hubbert got the credit he was due.

This theory of oil production has been applied to gold mining production. Some have proposed that gold production will at some point hit it peak. Lets look at U.S. gold mine production from the U.S. Geological Survey(3,4,5,6, 7,8,9):

1993 = 331 tons

1994 = 327 tons

1995 = 317 tons

1996 = 326 tons

1997 = 362 tons

1998 = 366 tons

1999 = 341 tons

2000 = 353 tons

2001 = 335 tons

2002 = 298 tons

2003 = 277 tons

2004 = 258 tons

2005 = 256 tons

2006= 252 tons

2007= 238 tons

2008 = 233 tons

2009 = 223 tons

2010 = 231 tons

2011 = 234 tons

2012 = 235 tons

2013 = 230 tons

2014 = 211 tons (estimate)

so we see that over a 20 year period, the United States mine production fell from 327 tons in 1994 to only 211 tons in 2014. As 2014 was an estimate by the U.S. Geological Survey, lets look at 1993 to 2013. The U.S. mine industry mined 331 tons of gold in 1993 versus only 230 tons in 2013., 20 years later. That's *101 tons less* gold mined. This calculates to a 30.5% reduction of mine output.

Surely in 20 years, technology had to improve somewhat in the mining industry to get more gold out. Maybe it wasn't economic? Lets look at the price of gold between 1993 and 2013. We'll use the middle of the years. On June.15, 1993 the price of gold was $365.35 per ounce. On June.14,2013 (the 15th was a Saturday) the price was $1,391.25.(10).

So the price of gold increased over $1,000 per ounce in this period! The $1,391.25 was not even the highest price, either, lest I be accused of only seeking out the highest price. Gold had topped $1,900 per ounce in august of 2011. The price change between 1993 and 2013 represents a 280.78% increase.

I think we can put the economic reasons to bed for the decrease in production. Most of the large corporate gold miners in the U.S. are publicly traded companies. They have a fiduciary responsibility to their shareholders to increase profits. It's not central planning like the old

USSR here. They would be grabbing that gold to cash in as fast as they possibly could. I deliberately used a very long period of 20 years here, so that naysayers can't say that "well, it can take years of investment in equipment to bring up production". Over 20 years, this argument doesn't hold up at all. Examining the evidence we have, it certainly seems like Peak Gold has come to the United States. Owning a gold mine just isn't what it used to be...at least in the U.S.

What about the whole world? For 2013 mine production was 2,800 tons of gold, with a world reserve of 55,000 tons. (of which 3000 tons in the U.S.)(3). For 1995 (oldest data available for the world through the US Geological Survey) world mine production was 2,250 tons of gold with a world reserve of 46,000 tons (of which 5600 tons in the U.S.)(12). This data tells us 2 important things. First, the world production of gold was able to be increased from 2,250 to 2,800, an increase of 24.44%. while reserves went from being listed at 46,000 tons to 55,000 tons as new discoveries were made and the much higher gold price made mining more economical. The second point is that the United States has lost both production AND reserves. U.S. reserves went from 5,600 tons to 3,000 tons. The United States' gold reserves have declined by almost half, even with higher prices to spur exploration and production. This adds further credibility to the idea that the U.S. has already reached "Peak Gold" and now is in its decline phase.

It is interesting to note that the gold that is being mined now seems to be a lot harder to get to then the past. All the low lying fruit was mined decades if not centuries ago. Look at Barrick, one of the world's largest gold miners with operations around the world. On their home page(11), it states that their production guidance for 2015 are "...at all-in sustaining costs of $830-$870 per ounce..." It goes on to say that "our five core mines in the Americas are forecast to contribute 60-65% of overall production this year at all-in sustaining costs of $700-$725 per ounce" if we go back and look at the1998 annual report of Barrick, it states that their "cash operating costs per ounce" was only $160 (and for 1997 $182).

So gold prices are way up, but the costs of extracting gold are way up also. If Barrick had been able to keep costs per ounce under wraps, they would have been making money hand over fist right now. This *isn't* the case. My theory is that as gold prices increase, the large gold mining companies open more mines and start processing ore that isn't as good which drives the cost part of the equation up through the roof. To be fair to Barrick and the industry, this is kind of what they have to do to stay in the business. It's similar to oil companies – as oil prices go up, they have to go where the oil is, such as in the frozen tundra of Alaska or doing ultra deep drilling offshore on platforms, or in dealing with crazy dictator types in banana republics. I'm sure they don't *want* to do any of this if they had a choice – it's far more expensive and dangerous for their workers, but it's what they must do to get the oil. And so it seems for gold.

Some will argue that gold is totally different than oil because oil is used up when burned and gold is not. Gold can be and is recovered after use. This is true, and a very good argument. Peak gold has to do with mining production, but how will recycling affect the equation? Lets think about this qualitatively for a moment. We've all seen those television commercials telling us to send in our unwanted gold for cash, especially when the price is rising. But once people get rid of their unwanted and unloved jewelry, what then? This seems to be one of those one time things people do. We can look up how much gold exists already in the world, but let's be honest with ourselves here. That rare gold coin in mint state worth thousands isn't a candidate to be recycled. You're probably not going to rip out your tooth to get at the gold in a gold filling. Those engagement rings and wedding bands I'm certain are off limits. So I think that it is misleading to assume all gold out there is available to potentially be recycled. It technically is, but in reality it just isn't.

Chapter 3 - Gold – The "useless" metal – Its Weakness or Strength?

Although gold has been used extensively for the last thousands of years, it is rather amazing that the demand has been for the same kind of uses. In our modern age, commodities of all types have evolved to a large degree from ancient times. Iron Ore can make steel. Wood - it's not just for burning anymore. It can be made into everything from houses to No.2 pencils. Sand can make glass. Whole materials have been synthetically created such as plastics using oil as feedstock. Basically, modern technology has revisited ancient commodities, and while still using them for ancient purposes, has also found all kinds of new applications for them *and* higher level products which satisfy our more advanced way of life.

This is decidedly *not* the case with gold. What did people use gold for back millennia ago? They used it as money in the form of coins. They used it to store their wealth in hoards. They used it to decorate themselves and their prized possessions. Those were the main uses in ancient civilizations for gold

How about now? What do people use gold for? Here are the demand figures for gold from the World Gold Council:(1)

Tonnes	2013	2014
Jewelry	**2,669.1**	**2,461.4**
Technology	**354.3**	**346.4**
--Electronics	248.6	277.5

--Other Industrial	82.7	49.0
--Dentistry	23.0	19.9
Investment	**784.8**	**819.1**
Total Bar & Coin Demand	1,700.8	1,002.2
Physical bar demand	1,334.8	725.40
Official Coin	266.1	204..5
Medals/Imitation Coin	99.8	72.2
ETFs & similar products	-915.9	-183.1
Central Banks & other inst.	**625.5**	**590.5**
GOLD DEMAND:	**4,433.7**	**4,217.4**
LBMA Gold price US $/OZ	**$1,411.2**	**$1,266.40**

Surprisingly, even with all the advances in technology, gold has not found much industrial use. Demand has remained Jewelry (decorating ourselves) as the largest use. Followed by a large amount of Investment demand & wealth storage (Central bank demand is really a type of investment and wealth preservation. It is listed separately from the investment column, but most people would classify it to be a type of investment, albeit on a different level compared to individual investors). That's it – the lion's share of uses are jewelry and as investment/store of wealth. Technology (Industrial demand) represented only 7.99% in 2013, and only 8.21% in 2014.

Because of this lack of industrial demand, people that have only a peripheral understanding of the precious metals market often come to the conclusion that gold is thus "useless". Some make the leap that because gold is "useless", it should not be worth a lot of money. These people are using the same line of reasoning that some used back in 1971, when the U.S. dollar was officially separated from gold by President Nixon, thus ending any form of gold backed currency. Back in 1971, some thought that by breaking the link between the dollar and gold, gold would sink in value. These people made a faulty assumption. They assumed that the dollar was holding up the value of gold. They had it completely backwards. It was in fact the gold that was holding up the value of the dollar. From 1971, gold has skyrocketed in price. Sure, its had ups and downs but the long term trend is a rising gold price. The dollar on the other hand did not fare so well. It was the dollar which plunged in value.

The truth is, the people who think because gold is "useless" and therefore should not be worth a great deal have too simple an understanding of gold. Gold is actually very useful – just not useful in industry. Industrial use is tied to industry. Industry is tied to the economy as a whole. And we all know how the economy can be awfully fickle. It's good one year, a disaster for the next couple years, then back to being great again. The economy is always in flux, always bouncing around see-sawing between growing and recession. Industry booms and busts right along with how the economy is doing.

If you want to invest along the lines of how the economy and industry are doing, the stock market as a whole is usually a good proxy. There is a technical measure of this correlation – it's called "beta".

Some technical info: Beta is "a measure of a fund's sensitivity to market movements" "the beta of the market is 1.00 by definition. "a beta of 1.10 shows that the fund has performed 10% better than its benchmark index in up markets and 10% worse in down markets, assuming all other factors remain constant. Conversely, a beta of 0.85 indicates that the fund's excess return is expected to perform 15% worse than the market's excess return during up markets and 15% better during down markets"(2)

Beta is calculated not only for funds, but for individual stocks as well. Most stocks have a positive number, meaning that they move with the rest of the market to some degree. Very few investments have a negative beta. Gold is an investment that is generally considered to have either a negative beta or a very low beta number. This means that its performance is usually inverse to the market. Meaning that most times gold performs opposite of the market. Usually, gold is expected to move higher when the market as a whole is going down. Gold usually is expected to lose value when a market is rising. I say "usually expected" because beta is based on past performance, so it is not a perfect predictor of what is to come. It is not a crystal ball. Morningstar notes: "A specialty fund that invests primarily in gold, for example, will usually have a low beta, as its performance is tied more closely to the price of gold and gold-mining stocks than to the overall market"(2) (Author's note: in my experience gold mining stocks are NOT a good substitute for physical gold, as they often behave more like stock in general than precious metals.).

To look at how this plays out in real life, let's compare how stocks and gold behaved in various years. The S&P 500 is a widely recognized benchmark to gauge the stock market as a whole. Compare the yearly performance of the S&P 500 (3) against gold's yearly performance (4) in terms of price change:

Year	S&P 500	Gold
1997	up 33.10%	down 22.21%
1998	up 28.34%	up 0.57%
1999	up 20.89%	up 0.54%
2000	down 9.03%	down 6.06%
2001	down 11.85%	up 1.41%
2002	down 21.97%	up 23.96%
2003	up 28.36%	up 21.74%
2004	up 10.74%	up 4.40%
2005	up 4.83%	up 17.77%
2006	up 15.61%	up 23.92%
2007	up 5.48%	up 31.59%
2008	down 36.55%	up 3.97%
2009	up 25.94%	up 25.04%
2010	up 14.82%	up 30.60%
2011	up 2.10%	up 7.80%
2012	up 15.89%	up 8.68%
2013	up 32.15%	down 27.60%
2014	up 13.52%	down 0.4%

We can see that many times the price movements are different between stocks and gold. In some years, both gold and stocks were up or down together. However, for the years in which stocks are far down, gold is usually up. This is mostly the result of investors moving away from stocks and into what they consider a safe haven. Likewise, when stocks are on a tear and surging higher, gold declines in price as investors take money out of gold and pile into stocks. This illustrates the concept of beta.

So, if gold enjoyed more industrial demand, it would start living and dying by the vagaries of industry in general. Gold is actually more prized because it is *not* affected by the booms and busts of industry. People seek out gold to counter-balance a portfolio heavy in stocks and bonds. Its "industrial uselessness" is actually a prized virtue.

Chapter 4 - Money Talks - What does our money tell us by looking at it?

When we look at money, what does it say to us? Money, in all its forms, contains information. Whether we are looking at current issue U.S. Currency, historic silver or gold coins, even foreign money, one thing remains clear – nations endeavor to use whatever real estate is available on the money to convey certain messages. Themes emerge that tell the holder a story. Most notably are the themes of shared values and religion, patriotism, ideas and ideals, and history. What do the messages tell us about the issuing government? What does it tell us about ourselves and what we hold dear?

When looking at United States money, there remains some similarities between our historic pieces versus the modern issues we handle daily. At its most basic, they both showcase prominently the face amount. This is vital information, but even this bit of info can be subtly different. Take a $20 bill as an example. Both the paper currency we use today as well as the historic "gold certificate" (paper currency backed by gold coin) spell out "Twenty Dollars" on them as well as featuring a numerical "20" in each corner of the bill. The gold coin does not use any numerals on them. The twenty dollar gold coin says "TWENTY DOLLARS" on the back of the coin only. Older versions of the coin – (minted in 1876 and before) say only "TWENTY D." on the bottom of the back of the coin. Why is that? Perhaps, when you're holding up a heavy hunk of gold in the palm of your hand, it is just instinctively understood by the holder that this has real value. Because gold has existed as a preferred form of money for 1,000's of years, the face value only needed the most cursory explanation of face value. You didn't have to try hard to convince people of its worth. It's altogether different with paper money. If anything, the paper devotes a whole lot of surface area simply spelling out its "assigned value". This is true even for the gold-backed paper – They are emblazoned with a gold colored seal on the front of the note and the serial numbers are gold colored as well. Even though this paper was gold-backed, the government went out of their way to convince people that it really was as good as the gold coin in the palm of the hand. So paper money has always had a lot more emphasis on trying to convince the holder that it was in fact worth something, even in the days when it was freely convertible to the actual gold. This is a subtle difference, but considering that it's the most basic information, an interesting difference.

How about a not so subtle difference: Let's consider the image of who or what is on our money. Starting with the current day on the front side of our coins and paper bills: President George Washington is on our $1 bill and quarter. President Thomas Jefferson is on our $2 bill and the nickel. President Abraham Lincoln is on the $5 bill and the penny. Secretary of the Treasury Alexander Hamilton is on our $10 bill. President Andrew Jackson is on our $20 bill. President Ulysses S. Grant is on our $50 bill. Elder Statesman Benjamin Franklin is on the $100 bill. President Franklin D. Roosevelt is on our dime. President John F. Kennedy is on our half dollar (yes, they are still minted!). Various U.S. presidents are on the front of the $1 coin (yes, they are still minting a dollar coin! And NO – it is not real gold, just gold-colored!). Notice that the vast majority are historic U.S. presidents. I love America and American history, but these presidents were all rulers of our country during their tenure.

Gold coins minted for use as money never had rulers on them. In fact, they were amazingly consistent in who was on the front – Lady Liberty was on every single $20 gold coin minted. There were different images – showing the head profile or showing her walking, but it was always *her* on the coin. She was also on every $10, $5, and $2.50 gold coin minted before 1908. On these lower denomination gold coins, Native American Indian heads were on the front starting in 1908. This should tell us something about how people thought back then. The ideal of Liberty was on people's minds, and this trumped the importance of any ruler, no matter how significant their contribution. The Liberty head designs were on the silver coins and copper pennies as well. It wasn't just limited to the gold coins. The hostile Native Americans had all been killed off by 1908, so I guess it was in vogue to be friendly to Native Americans, now that so many of them were dead and displaced from their lands.

How about the back of our money? The old gold coins of the $2.50, $5, $10, and $20 all had some incarnation of an American eagle on the backside. Amazingly consistent – it shows the patriotism and ideals people had for the country.

What's on the backs of our money today? The $1 bill has the great seal of the United States. The $2 bill portrays Trumbull's painting of the signing of the Declaration of Independence. The $5 bill has the Lincoln Memorial. The $10 bill shows the U.S. Treasury. The $20 bill shows the White House. The $50 bill shows the United States Capitol. The $100 bill shows Independence hall. Of our coins: The Penny shows the Union Shield. The Nickel shows Monticello. The dime shows an olive branch, a torch, and an oak branch. The quarter shows various designs depicting scenes and symbols from around the country. The half dollar shows the Presidential Seal. The $1 coin shows the Statue of Liberty (Liberty finally made a comeback on one of our modern coins! She's in the form of a statue, and relegated to the backside of a coin we almost never see or use, but still...some progress!).

What we see is that many of these reverse side images depict the bases of power where our rulers rule from. Images of the White House, Capitol Building, and the Treasury may stir our American Patriotism, but they also sublimely remind us of the importance of those in power. Other images, such as Monticello and the Lincoln Memorial pay homage to past presidents. There's nothing really "wrong" with any of this....but it does make one wonder about our priorities and what matters most to us in our lives. Every time our presidential election cycle comes up, people begin getting concerned with the possibility of their liberties being trampled on or restricted or taken away outright. When was the last presidential election, when at least a sizeable number of Americans didn't start fearing for their Second Amendment rights to keep and bear arms? What about the First Amendment, the right to free speech and press? It's common to hear people speak of how the liberal media is biased to the left; the mainstream media is controlled by a handful of giant corporations; and the Internet may be monitored by the government. The people living 100+ years ago were clearly taken by the whole concept of liberty. They must have been, since it was the image on almost all the money circulating back then. And here we all are...worrying about losing our liberty with the next election cycle. And yet the image of Liberty herself is virtually absent on our money of today. It's either a strange coincidence or something much more sinister by design has been planned.

Our money carries the words "In God We Trust". This came about during the Civil War, when the motto was added to the coinage. "largely because of the increased religious sentiment that existed during the Civil War...in a letter dated November 13, 1861 ...written to Secretary Chase by Rev. M.R. Watkinson, Minister of the Gospel from Ridleyville, Pennsylvania, and read in part "Dear Sir, You are about to submit your annual report to the Congress respecting the affairs of the national finances. One fact touching our currency has hitherto been seriously overlooked. I mean the recognition of the Almighty God in some form on our coins". It took three years for Congress to respond...An Act of Congress, approved on April 11, 1864 authorized the coinage of the two-cent coins on which the motto first appeared. "(2)

We can learn a couple of things from this. Congress moved slow even back then. More important is that at a time when Americans lay dead by the tens of thousands on the battlefields, people recognized the need to proclaim their faith in God for all the world to see. In addition to support from clergy, it had popular support. "The motto was omitted from the new gold coins issued in 1907, causing a storm of public criticism. As a result, legislation passed in May 1908 made "In God We Trust" mandatory on all coins on which it had previously appeared...Legislation approved in 1955 made the appearance of "In God We Trust" mandatory on all coins and paper currency of the United States...On July 30, 1956, by an Act of Congress, "In God We Trust" became the national motto of the United States"(2). This shows the level of support this motto had with people, throughout different generations. It also shows how the "silent majority" can stand up and force the government to acquiesce to the people's will.

Let's think about denominations. Specifically, our very lowest – the penny. It's sort of like the building block of the money supply. The way atoms are tiny but make up every single object around us, so too does the penny. The one cent piece gets no respect. A lot of people would not go through the hassle of even bending over to pick one up off the ground. What has happened to Benjamin Franklin's advice that "a penny saved is a penny earned"? Well, for starters, a penny in the time of Benjamin Franklin was worth a lot more than it is today. Maybe if Franklin was alive today, he would be substituting a "dollar" or "fiver" in place of the penny in his saying.

Most pennies are not truly in circulation per se. They are kept in coin jars and tins in people's homes. People rarely touch these jars until they finally get around to either wrapping them or bringing them to a coin counting machine. Then the purpose is to exchange them for a few dollars...to get some "real" spending money. Many stores have "take a penny/leave a penny" cups. Nobody really wants to deal with them. They're a hassle. To get enough of them to buy anything of any value takes so many of them that nobody would want to lug them around in their pocket.

Canada decided to eliminate the penny from their economy back in 2012. While the pennies can still be spent, the government will no longer mint them. They say it will save the taxpayers $11 million per year.(1). The Canadian Mint says that in commerce, if no pennies are available, the price is either rounded up or down to the nearest 5 cent price point.

In the United States, the penny is still being made. It actually costs more than 1 cent to mint a penny. This is even true now that the penny has been debased. The penny isn't even made of copper anymore. The last copper pennies (95% copper) were minted back in 1982. Also in 1982 and onward, pennies were, and are, produced with 97.5% Zinc and only 2.5% copper. This worked OK back then, but now the prospect of our government making pennies is a losing proposition. I'm not even saying we should stop making the penny. The coin collector in me feels nostalgic for these one cent pieces. I think instead, the penny is destined be made out of an even cheaper metal such as steel in the future to save even more money.

The *reason* I think the penny will not be scrapped has more to do with perception. I believe that the government does not want to stop producing them, even if it has to lose money in the process. The reasoning is simple: The day they stop making them is the day they have to admit they are basically worthless...and thus, the dollar itself has become almost worthless. This simple line of thinking is a dangerous idea. It has such profound ramifications that no politician would want to take on. By association, the government would almost have to admit that the Federal Reserve has done such a lousy job managing our money that our money supply has plummeted in value. It would expose our money itself as a fraud. When thinking of these consequences, it's easy to see why the government will continue to pump out pennies by the billions each year. Even if it doesn't make any financial sense, it keeps the illusion going that our money is valuable, and that's good enough for the government.

Chapter 5 - American Civil War

The American Civil war was one of the exception periods in the United States' otherwise sound money system. The U.S. was fighting for its life, so there was definitely an emergency of great proportions. The U.S. had effectively lost nearly half the country to the rebels. Philosophically, even the labels of the combatants bears significance in the fight. The southerners who broke away called their new country The Confederate States of America, thus the "Confederates". The north was "The Union" which was the United States of America. History books talk of the Confederate Army and Union Army, but in the north this is not exactly how all people saw it. Many northerners saw only the United States (the Union) as being a legitimate nation, and refused to really recognize the southern Confederate government. To many, they were just rebels.

Whatever the semantics, the U.S. was in for a very big fight, which rested squarely on the shoulders of the United States Army, which had never been tested on a scale like this before. At the beginning of the war – "In July 1861 the two armies were nearly equal in strength with less than 200,000 soldiers on each side; however at the peak of troop strength in 1863, union soldiers outnumbered Confederate soldiers by a ratio of 2 to 1. The size of union forces in January 1863 totaled over 600,000. Two years later, that number had not changed dramatically for the Union Army but had dropped to about 200,000 for the Confederate army"(1). So even in 1865 as the war was ending, the rebels still had a 200,000 strong army. It just shows the immense size of the problem that had to be dealt with.

We can see that the United States coined many more gold coins as part of its effort to pay for the war. To get a sense, lets examine gold denominations minted around this time by year. The mintage(2):

For the $20 gold coin "double eagle" from all mints combined:

1857 = 1,439,875

1858 = 1,093,674

1859 = 689,142

1860 = 1,129,220

1861 = 3,749,453

1862 = 946,306

1863 = 1,109,360

1864 = 997,945

1865 = 1,393,700

For the $10 gold coin "eagle" from all mints combined:

1857 = 48,106

1858 = 34,321

1859 = 25,400

1860 = 28,383

1861 = 128,733

1862 = 23,495

1863 = 11,248

1864 = 6,080

1865 = 20,705

For the $5 gold coin "half eagle" from all mints combined:

1857 = 246,594

1858 = 87,954

1859 = 71,887

1860 = 70,473

1861 = 657,926

1862 = 13,965

1863 = 19,472

1864 = 8,108

1865 = 28,907

We can see that by far the United States produced more gold coins in 1861 than any of the recent years before or after. We can draw some conclusions from this. First, this corresponds with 1861 being the outbreak of the Civil War. No doubt that the United States felt they would need to spend much more government money on paying troops, munitions, and all manner of war supplies. It is interesting that the U.S. did not continue producing massive quantities of gold coins all the way through the war years. After 1861 the war only intensified – the U.S. bulked up their army as did the Confederates. There clearly would have been a need for more money in the economy both for the government to spend and for providing liquidity in the private sector. Everything points to having the need for the mint to pump out many more gold coins like they did in 1861. There was a demand for the gold coins...but perhaps they just couldn't accomplish this.

Some astute readers with knowledge of coins may point out that the U.S. had lost the mints that were located in the south to the Confederates. This is absolutely true. The Confederacy seized the mints at New Orleans, Louisiana, Charlotte, North Carolina, and Dahlonega, Georgia. Losing three mints, one might expect that this loss would crimp the United State's production capacity, especially since 1861 was their last year of contributing. You would be wrong with this line of reasoning. Both the mints at Charlotte and Dahlonega only produced gold coins, but in very small quantities. Also both these mints produced only the smaller gold coins - $5 half eagles and under. They did not produce the $10 eagle or $20 double eagle. The New Orleans mint was much larger. It had a much wider variety of output which included both gold and silver coinage. However, New Orleans did not produce gold coins in large amounts. The New Orleans mint's production loss would be felt, but mostly in the silver coinage they used to produce, especially half dollars and quarters. When examining gold coin production, especially the larger denominations, the United States' other mints in Philadelphia and San Francisco were both large and had the production capacity to ramp up and offset the loss of the three southern mints. Production capacity was not the reason for the lowered mintage figures for the rest of the war.

The massive production in 1861 may well have taken all the available gold stocks and even though the U.S. government wanted (and needed) to produce more, the U.S. just didn't have the gold to do it. This sets the stage for what came next: "paper money".

"In 1861, when the costs of the Civil War were swallowing the federal gold stock, the United States suspended dollar redemption. Instead of a convertible dollar, the Union issued a paper note, the infamous "greenback""(3). What made the new paper money "infamous" was the fact that people did not exactly like a new form of money shoved at them. People had been quite used to honest and sound money backed by specie (gold and silver) at this point. The Continental currency system that ended so badly was generations removed. The people living during the Civil War period had grown up with sound money from the government all their lives. People in the U.S. probably understood the need the government had, but it did not make it any easier to accept.

The fact is that people didn't fully accept it. The government printed a good amount of paper money "...Congress also issued $450 million in "greenbacks," paper money not backed by gold, to pay for the war. ("The Constitution, though implying the federal government should not issue paper money, did not expressly ban it.")(4). President Lincoln's administration sought loans from the major banks, mostly in New York City. The banks wanted interest rates in the range of 24% to 36%.(5) President Lincoln refused to borrow on such terms. These high rates of interest on offer further prove how weak the United States was perceived to be.

People weren't stupid back then – they knew what the spirit of the Constitution was getting at – that gold and silver were money, period. There did exist bank notes issued by private banks before the Civil War...publishers of the time actually printed books detailing how much each particular issue was actually worth. They were guaranteed by only the strength of the individual bank that printed it. "These bank notes were usually backed by gold or silver; if asked, banks were obliged to exchange specie for their paper"(4) Some were sound, some were not at all solvent. The bank notes were traded on their perceived value and safety versus just on the face value on the note – and these were supposed to be backed by gold or silver at that. There was definitely a speculative element to accept these private bank notes.

People must have been dismayed to see the government resort to the same kind of shenanigans. The government all the while kept on minting gold coins to use at the same time as the paper greenbacks that were not backed by anything at all – just the faith in the United States.

And that faith began to waiver. The degree depended on how good or bad the war was progressing at any particular moment. The U.S. government had already lost the whole south, so the U.S was immediately a smaller country from the start. At the beginning of the war, many people thought the war would last only months. The south inherited many disadvantages but were blessed to have some remarkably skilled generals leading their army. Nobody more so than their military leader General Robert E. Lee.

General Lee actually launched two invasions of the north during the Civil War. The first was when Lee took

50,000 confederate troops into Maryland in September 1862. This culminated with the battle of Antietam in Maryland on September 17, 1862. The confederates lost this battle, but this site is only 30 miles from Washington DC. If the Confederates succeeded, they were definitely close enough to have threatened the U.S. Capitol. The second invasion occurred in the summer of 1863. General Lee had defeated the U.S Army at the battles of Fredericksburg and Chancellorsville among others and thought it was time to invade the U.S. again. President Abraham Lincoln was frustrated with the way the war was progressing and kept changing generals at the top. General Lee invaded Pennsylvania with his roughly 70,000 troops. This resulted in the battle of Gettysburg against about 90,000 U.S. troops. The Confederate invasion was stopped at Gettysburg.

The point isn't to recite a history lesson from a high school history class here. Rather it is to show how money based on faith can be a very fickle thing. We sometimes feel the U.S. now is so strong as to be nearly invincible. This was not at all true back then. The war was dragging on longer than anyone had expected. The U.S Army suffered defeats down south and to top it all off, the rebels not only still existed, but were strong enough to launch actual invasions of their own. Add to this the fact that the British were somewhat sympathetic to the Confederate cause. The British sent 11,000 troops to Canada to protect their interests. Taken all together, things were a mess for the United States. Faith was in short supply. The result was that the U.S. paper money traded at a discount to gold bullion. Even now, if you were selling something, for $10, you would rather a $10 gold coin over a paper $10 bill. This is exactly the situation people faced back then. Only back then, the gold did trade hands, unlike today.

Sellers wanted gold more. Buyers wanted to keep their gold and trade their paper. There was a classic supply and demand imbalance when looking only at the face value amount printed on the note or stamped on the coin. Whenever an imbalance happens, something must adjust to reflect true supply and demand. This is exactly what happened back then. The paper money varied widely from being worth $131 to $100 in gold in 1863 after the Union won Gettysburg all the way down to $258 to $100 in gold in 1864 as the war dragged on. (6) It was always in flux and depended on individual people cutting their deals with one another. The take home is just because the government said that a particular piece of paper was worth x number of dollars doesn't make it so in real life.

Chapter 6 - Fed up with The Fed

The Federal Reserve came into being in 1913, under the guise of helping with panics such as the panic of 1907. It was a system devised to bring liquidity into the markets to deal with panics and liquidity crisis. When everyone ran to the bank to get out their money, and there wasn't enough money to go around, the Federal Reserve was supposed to step in and provide loans to the banks, as the "lender of last resort". The interest charged to the banks was punitively high, as a sort of punishment for not keeping enough cash on hand to satisfy demand.

The whole effort to establish a central bank was a conspiracy from day one. "The mustachioed man in the silk top hat strode to his private railcar parked at a New Jersey train station...Five more men –and a legion of porters and servants –soon joined him. They referred to each other by their first names only, an uncommon informality in 1910, intended to give the staff no hints as to who the men actually were, lest rumors make their way to the newspapers and then to the trading floors of New York and London. One of the men, a German immigrant named Paul Warburg, carried a shotgun in order to look like a duck hunter, despite having never drawn a bead on a waterfowl in his life. Two days later, the car deposited the men at the small Georgia port town of Brunswick, where they boarded a boat for the final leg of their journey. Jekyll Island, their destination, was a private resort owned by the powerful banker J.P. Morgan and some of his friends...Their host-the man in the silk top hat – was Nelson Aldrich, one of the most powerful senators of the day, a lawmaker who lorded over financial matters in the burgeoning nation. For nine days, working all day and into the night, the six men debated how to reform the banking and monetary systems of the United States...Secrecy was paramount. "Discovery" wrote one attendee later, "simply must not happen, or else all our time and effort would have been wasted. If it were to be exposed publicly that our particular group had gotten together and written a banking bill, that bill would have no chance whatever of passage by Congress"""(18). This quote proves that even one of their own members of this group, the so called "First Name Club" knew if the public got wind of this there would be outrage among the people, and none of the congressmen would vote for the bill which ended up being the Federal Reserve Act. This also proves that the effort was not on the up and up from the very beginnings to create the Fed.

The whole group of who these men were at Jekyll island were "Senator Aldrich, H.P. Davison of J.P. Morgan Company, Paul Warburg of Kuhn, Loeb Company, Frank Vanderlip of the National City Bank, and Charles D. Norton of the First National Bank."(14)

"Much of the influence exerted to get the Federal Reserve Act passed was done behind the scenes, principally by two shadowy, non-elected persons: The German immigrant, Paul Warburg, and Colonel Edward Mandell House of Texas."(14)

At the time, people in the U.S. were not happy with Wall Street and blamed the big New York banks for the panic of 1907. "The press seriously demanded that the New York banking monopoly be broken by turning over the administration of the new banking system to the most knowledgeable banker of them all, Paul Warburg."(14)

Paul Warburg was no doubt knowledgeable, but whose side was he on? "The Reichsbank, the central bank which controlled money and credit in Germany, and whose principle stockholders, were the Rothschilds and Paul Warburg's family banking house M. M. Warburg Company."(15)

The Rothschild family was (and still is) a banking dynasty in Europe. They were and are known to be extremely powerful and secretive. One of their branches in England, N. M. Rothschild & Sons actually would set the world price of gold every single day from their offices in London. This practice continued until 2004. Even today, when the price of gold is quoted, people refer to the price as the "London fix". This gives a snapshot of their immense power. Just have a look at what the family patriarch proclaimed back in the early 19th Century: "Because of his success in his speculations, Baron Nathan Mayer de Rothschild, as he now called himself, reigned as the supreme financial power in London. He arrogantly exclaimed, during a party in his mansion, "I care not what puppet is placed upon the throne of England to rule the Empire on which the sun never sets. The man who controls Britain's money supply controls the British Empire, and I control the British money supply."(19). It is amazing how little has been written about the Rothschilds for such a powerful family. As an example, Mr. Aldrich went to England when studying the central banks of Europe: "The Aldrich mission docked at Plymouth, England, on August 10, 1908, and was welcomed to dinner at Morgan's London home, with Lord Rothschild present".(21). This is in a book detailing how the Federal Reserve came to be, but there is very little information given about this family. Interestingly, a Rothschild is "present" with Aldrich and JP Morgan. We find that the Rothschilds play this secrecy game very well.

They manage to keep their names out of the press and the public eye, but they are there, lurking, with the top decision makers. My own guess is that they are not just quiet bystanders. I think it is the Rothschilds who are actually calling the shots.

Why do I think that? We have to understand the history of how J.P. Morgan, the man, came to be powerful in the first place. Eustace Mullins gives an incredibly detailed account in his book (19) Here is an ultra short version: In the early 1800's George Peabody, a banker goes to London. He is sought out by Baron Nathan Mayer de Rothschild, a powerful banker. Mr. Rothschild tells him that the Rothschild family in England is hated and not trusted by the wealthy aristocracy. He offers to set Mr Peabody up and bankroll him with Rothschild money. He gives Mr Peabody instructions to throw party's, as a way to get the rich families to like him and do business with him. Mr Peabody accepts and George Peabody & Co. goes on to make itself very rich and successful (they were being backed by the uber rich Rothschilds after all, but nobody knew this). Mr Peabody used Junius Morgan as his American agent. In 1854, Junius joins Peabody in London. Peabody had no kids to take over the firm. In 1864 Peabody retires, and Junius Morgan takes over the firm and names it Junius S Morgan & Co, in London. He starts using his own son J.P. Morgan as his American agent. In 1890, Junius dies, and his son takes over everything – American and English interests and renames the firm J.P. Morgan & Co. So J.P. Morgan & Co. began under the name George Peabody & Co with Rothschild backing. And we know that in 1908, here was Aldrich, Morgan, and a Rothschild all meeting for dinner at Morgan's England home...how cozy! (this would explain why when J.P. Morgan himself died Morgan left behind an estate worth about $80 million (equal to nearly $2 billion today), and on hearing of this sum, oil baron John D. Rockefeller was heard to quip, "and to think, he wasn't even a rich man."(23) Well, not nearly as rich as everyone thought...because a lot of what his company was thought to own was really his client's (the Rothschilds). This same article also states "Morgan's merchant bank was initially meant as a conduit for wealthy Europeans to invest in American business interests. This deep early connection to European interests would be of lifelong benefit to Morgan"(23).

This explains why some people such as Senator Owen made the connection that Morgan was really an agent for the powerful Rothschild family of England. (For some reason the Rothschild family was hated in England. Maybe they learned something from that experience and didn't want to be hated here in America as well. Or, maybe it was more practical – if the American public openly saw European bankers trying to wrest control of our nation's money supply, it would have been too much. The people would never have stood for it). Either way, the Rothschilds had already been on the receiving end of what it's like to be disliked by Americans just a short while earlier, in 1895.

In 1895, gold had been flowing out of the U.S. government's vaults to foreign countries as a result of a trade imbalance. The gold stock had gone down to dangerously low levels. "...only $9 million in gold coin remained in government vaults on Wall Street..."(J.P. Morgan spoke to President Cleveland) saying he knew of a $10-million draft about to be presented. "If that draft is presented, you can't meet it...It will be all over before 3 o'clock""(24). Basically, the U.S. government would have been presented a demand for gold it did not have. It's as if the United States had written a check that it did not have the money to cover. This draft (check) would have bounced – the United States would have gone into default that very day. The President asked Morgan for suggestions.

Morgan laid out a plan. "The Morgan and Rothschild houses in New York and London would gather 3.5 million ounces of gold, at least half from Europe, in exchange for about $65 million worth of thirty-year gold bonds. He also promised that gold obtained by the government wouldn't flow out again. This was the showstopper that mystified the financial world – a promise to rig, temporarily, the gold market."(24)

The plan worked. "News of the Morgan-Rothschild operation was a sedative for the financial market. When the syndicate bonds were offered, on February 20, 1895, they sold out in two hours in London, in only twenty-two minutes in New York."(25)

You would think that with this all unfolding, the public would be happy, but not so much. "...the syndicate was a victim of its success. It took up the bonds at 104 ½, then sold them at an opening price of 112 ¼; they quickly soared to 119. For the cynical, this sudden appreciation proved the syndicate had cheated the government and underpriced the issue. The interest rate of 3% was thought extremely harsh. In just twenty-two minutes, the bankers had booked $6 or $7 million in profits.."(25). Morgan later claimed these amounts to be exaggerated.

Notwithstanding bond pricing and interest rates, the American people surely would have been thankful for the Rothschild participation, since it saved the government from defaulting. I find it interesting that the Americans were *not* thankful. They were the opposite. "The Populist uproar was furious and laced with anti-

Semitism because of the Rothschild participation. Populist rabble-rouser Mary Lease called President Cleveland a tool "of Jewish bankers and British gold." The New York World described the syndicate as a pack of "bloodsucking Jews and aliens" In his vehement denunciation in Congress, William Jennings Bryan asked the clerk to read Shylock's bond from The Merchant of Venice". Bryan always denied that his attacks pandered to anti-Semitism. Campaigning in 1896, he told Jewish Democrats in Chicago "Our opponents have sometimes tried to make it appear that we are attacking a race when we denounced the financial policy of the Rothschilds. But we are not; we are as much opposed to the financial policy of J. Pierpont Morgan as we are to the financial policy of the Rothschilds."(25)

Whether people were outraged and furious with the Rothschilds because they were Jewish, or because people simply hated all the powerful bankers as Mr. Bryan stated, cannot be known. It could have been some combination of the two factors. It almost doesn't really matter. The bottom line is that the Rothschilds were not embraced for saving America from collapse. They were instead resented for it. The Rothschilds may have taken note of this public feeling, and made a decision to stay in the shadows when dealing in America. And why not? They already had J.P. Morgan & Co to be their U.S. agent. They could largely conduct their American operations through him from this point forward. They could let Morgan take the brunt of the hate and insults, and they could simply reap the profits from their endeavors. I believe this 1895 incident was the turning point when the Rothschilds completely "went dark" and their operations in the U.S. became a secretive "black-ops" type endeavor.

Either way, "J.P. Morgan had been appointed head representative of the Rothschild interests in the United States...J.P. Morgan & Company of New York, Drexel & Company of Philadelphia, Grenfell & Company of London, and Morgan Harjes Cie of Paris, M.M. Warburg Company of Germany and America, and the House of Rothschild were all affiliated"(22)

Paul Warburg spoke to the House Banking and Currency Committee in 1913 and said "I am a member of the banking house of Kuhn, Loeb Company. I came over to this country in 1902, having been born and educated in the banking business in Hamburg, Germany, and studied banking in London and Paris, and have gone all around the world."(14). Is it just coincidence that Hamburg, London, and Paris were all strongholds of the Rothschild family's banking empire? I don't think so, as the Rothschild and Warburg families owned the central bank of Germany together.

Not everyone in Congress was in favor of the Federal Reserve Act. During a congressional appearance "...questioning allowed Mr. Schiff to talk for many minutes without revealing any information about the operations of the banking house of Kuhn, Loeb Company, of which he was senior partner, and which Senator Robert L. Owen had identified as the representative of the European Rothschilds in the United States"(14). He clearly saw through the smokescreen that Paul Warburg wasn't just acting on his own, but was indeed tied in with the Rothschilds.

Congressman Lindberg said "This Act establishes the most gigantic trust on earth. When the President signs this bill, the invisible government by the monetary power will be legalized. The people may not know it immediately, but the day of reckoning is only a few years removed. The trusts will soon realize that they have gone too far even for their own good".(14)

"To further confuse the American people and blind them to the real purpose of the proposed Federal Reserve Act, the architects of the Aldrich Plan, powerful Nelson Aldrich, although no longer a senator, and Frank Vanderlip, president of the National City Bank, set up a hue and cry against the bill. They gave interviews whenever they could find an audience denouncing the proposed Federal Reserve Act as inimical to banking and to good government. The bugaboo of inflation was raised because of the Act's provisions for printing Federal Reserve notes. The Nation, on October 23, 1913, pointed out , "Mr. Aldrich himself raised a hue and cry over the issue of government "fiat money", that is, money issued without gold or bullion back of it, although a bill to do precisely that had been passed in 1908 with his own name as author, and he knew besides , that the "government" had nothing to do with it, that the Federal Reserve Board would have full charge of issuing of such moneys."(14). Mr. Aldrich was using disinformation. This particular newspaper called him out on his past supporting a bill in 1908 that gave national banks the ability to issue emergency currency (while the bill passed, it never actually happened in practice as the 1907 panic had ended). The newspapers did not know (nor did anyone else) that Mr. Aldrich was one of the men at Jekyll Island crafting the Federal Reserve Act himself, which now he publicly went on record saying how he thought it a bad idea. This makes no sense, until you realize that Mr. Aldrich was a skilled politician. He got the ball rolling on the bill, and once it was getting ready to pass the Congress he could denounce it, so he could look like the good guy, watching out for the people. In fact, nobody would have suspected his involvement in crafting the bill because of his remarks.

All these powerful interests were able to get their way right before Christmas. "It was a long standing political courtesy that important legislation would not be acted upon during the week before Christmas, but this tradition was rudely shattered in order to perpetrate the Federal Reserve Act on the American people".(14). "Paul Warburg, who for several days had maintained a small office in the Capitol building, where he directed the successful pre-Christmas campaign to pass the bill, and where senators and congressmen came hourly at his bidding to carry out his strategy."(14). In politics, money talks. Paul Warburg was well endowed with money to spread around, so of course many politicians listened and complied with what he wanted. Call it an early 20th Century political PAC. Some congressmen went against this because they were patriots and did what was right for the American people, but there were not enough of them to stop the legislation from passing. "The unprecedented speed" with which the Federal Reserve Act had been passed by Congress...became known as the Christmas Massacre"(14)

Here is how The Federal Reserve defines their Purpose:(8)

The Federal Reserve System, often referred to as the Federal Reserve or simply "the Fed," is the central bank of the United States. It was created by the Congress to provide the nation with a safer, more flexible, and more stable monetary and financial system. The Federal

Reserve was created on December 23, 1913, when President Woodrow Wilson signed the Federal Reserve Act into law. Today, the Federal Reserve's responsibilities fall into four general areas.

- Conducting the nation's monetary policy by influencing money and credit conditions in the economy in pursuit of full employment and stable prices.
- Supervising and regulating banks and other important financial institutions to ensure the safety and soundness of the nation's banking and financial system and to protect the credit rights of consumers.
- Maintaining the stability of the financial system and containing systemic risk that may arise in financial markets.
- Providing certain financial services to the U.S. government, U.S. financial institutions, and foreign official institutions, and playing a major role in operating and overseeing the nation's payments systems.

Despite the name – The "Federal Reserve", it is *not* a part of the U.S. government. The Federal Reserve has 12 branches, or in their parlance 12 "districts" that corresponds to a number:

1. Boston
2. New York
3. Philadelphia
4. Cleveland
5. Richmond
6. Atlanta
7. Chicago
8. St. Louis

9. Minneapolis
10. Kansas City
11. Dallas
12. San Francisco

"These banks were and are "owned" by the commercial banks in their districts. Only member banks could directly use the services the Federal Reserve Banks would supply, but non-member banks could access them through their established correspondent arrangements with banks that did become members"(1). This network of bank branches is owned by private for-profit bank corporations. Even books that are favorable to the Fed do not deny this point. Roger Lowenstein's book "America's Bank" concedes that Mr. Warburg "argued that only "a modern central bank" could cure America's ills. By "modern" Warburg meant "European" – that is, managed by private bankers".(26)

Taken together they get to decide what the interest rates and what the money supply should be. It seems crazy, like some kind of fictional new world order story, except that it is true. You can see it on the U.S. $1 bill – take a look. The seal on the bill corresponds to the particular bank that issued it. The shares the commercial banks own entitle them to an annual 6% dividend, which is not too bad. After being paid this 6% dividend out of profits, the excess profits then go to the U.S. Treasury – this is like the big kick-back or bribe, for letting them operate. We have to understand that the real gem, the real power, isn't getting these fat dividends or bribing the government with big kick-backs to the Treasury department. The true power lies in owning and controlling the *whole system*: setting interest rates, creating money itself, and deciding the value of that money.

"To lower rates, the Fed (or any other central bank) creates money from nothing, a process called "printing money", even though it is electronic, and uses that money to buy U.S. Treasury securities from the portfolios of the banks. The banks then have fewer securities but more money to lend. This increased supply of money lowers the federal funds rate, the price of money. When the Fed wants to push up rates, it siphons money out of the market by selling government securities from its vast portfolio; this reduces the credit supply and raises the price of money. The Fed's balance sheet – its portfolio of government securities and loans on one side (its assets) and the reserves of the banks and currency in circulation on the other (its liabilities) – is part of the magic of central banking. Because the Fed can create money, it can buy as many bonds and make as many loans as it wants.."(2)

What in essence happened is that these private banks hijacked and took over our nation's money supply. Do we know that the collection of banks that own the Fed are going to do the "right thing" for our nation? If it comes down to doing what's right for the United States versus doing what will make the member banks more profit, then these for-profit banks that own the Fed are going to choose profit for themselves.

Who Owns The Fed?

The next logical question is – who are these banks that own the 12 member banks? The power of these banks are not all the same. The New York Fed (district 2) is by far the most powerful of the 12. "The Federal Reserve Bank of New York holds the majority of shares in the Federal Reserve System (53 percent)" (27). It manages to get what it wants even when opposed by the other districts "It should be noted that the NY Fed was the only Fed regional bank with much enthusiasm for big-bank bailouts. Other regional bank heads, including Stern, Dallas's Richard Fisher, Richmond's Jeff Lacker, and Kansas City's Thomas Hoenig, have been staunch critics"(12) (Mr. Stern was head of the Minneapolis Fed). We all know what happened – the biggest banks in the country got their massive bailouts during the Great Recession in 2009. The New York Fed couldn't be stopped even with "staunch" resistance from 4 other Fed districts. The combined power of Minneapolis, Dallas, Richmond, and the Kansas City Feds proved no match for when the New York Fed wanted to do something. Basically, the New York Fed is the undisputed King on the chess board, and all the other Feds are lesser pieces. So we would be especially interested in knowing exactly which banks own the New York Federal Reserve Bank....

So, I went in search of this answer. What I found was shocking – some of the federal reserve banks such as the fifth district in Richmond lay it all out nice and neat and easy to find on their website. How about that most important of all the Federal Reserve banks –

The New York Fed? Nothing. It simply says that they are owned by member banks, but does not go into any details. Over the years the New York Fed has been the subject of all kinds of conspiracy theories in terms of its ownership. ""(Eustace) Mullins and (Gary) Kah both argued that the Federal Reserve Bank of New York is owned by foreigners. Although the New York Fed is just one of twelve Federal Reserve Banks, controlling it, they claimed, is tantamount to control of the entire System".(3) I include this, to first just point out all the controversy that has surrounded the issue of who the owners (member banks) are of the New York Fed. The interesting thing to me is that they could dispel all the controversy by just making it public like the Richmond district does. I reached out to The New York Fed asking them to provide any information as to who the member banks are (I did not ask who owns the New York Fed, or who are the shareholders.). I simply phrased the request as a polite request asking who their member banks were (since this would tell us the answer of who owns them). I received no reply, and heard nothing in response. The omission on who these member banks are that owns them speaks volumes – the silence on their part is deafening. It begs the question from any rational person: If everything is on the up and up, why don't they just disclose this information?

In Mr. Eustace Mullin's book "the Secret of the Federal Reserve"(14), the author lists:

"The Federal Reserve Bank of New York issued 203,053 shares and as filed with the Comptroller of the Currency May 19, 1914, the large New York City banks took more than half the outstanding shares."

National City Bank = 30,000 shares (Rockefeller Kuhn,Loeb Controlled bank)

First National Bank = 15,000 shares (J.P. Morgan controlled bank)

Note: these two banks above merged in 1955, and thus would have owned nearly one fourth of the shares of the New York Fed.

National Bank of Commerce of New York City = 21,000 shares

Chase National Bank = 6,000 shares

The Marine Nation Bank of Buffalo = 6,000

"The Shareholders of these banks which own the stock of the Federal Reserve Bank of New York are the people who have controlled our political and economic destinies since 1914. They are the Rothschilds, of Europe, Lazard Freres (Eugene Meyer), Kuhn Loeb Company, Warburg Germany, Lehman Brothers, Goldman Sachs, the Rockefeller family, and the J.P. Morgan interests. These interests have merged and consolidated in recent years, so that the control is much more concentrated. National Bank of Commerce is now Morgan Guaranty Trust Company. Lehman Brothers has merged with Kuhn, Loeb Company First National Bank has merged with the National City Bank, and in the other eleven Federal Reserve Districts, These same shareholders indirectly own or control shares in those banks, with the other shares owned by the leading families in those areas who own or control the principal industries in these regions"(14). While this is certainly useful information, it is dated – first by the original holders being in 1914, and then secondly when Mr. Mullins' book came out in 1983 with revisions that spoke of the mergers.

In doing some digging in terms of how the New York Fed is controlled, here is what I found on the New York Fed's website(4)

There are 3 classes of directors that make up the 9 member board (3 from each class)

CLASS A DIRECTOR FACTS

Elected by member banks;
Elected to represent stockholding banks;
May be an officer, director or employee of a member bank; and
May not play a role in appointment of presidents or regulatory decisions.

CLASS B DIRECTOR FACTS

Elected by member banks;
Elected to represent the public;
Chosen with due but not exclusive consideration to the interests of agriculture, commerce, industry, services, labor and consumers; and
Cannot be officers, directors or employees of any bank.

CLASS C DIRECTOR FACTS

Appointed by the Federal Reserve Board;
Chosen to represent the public;
Chosen with due but not exclusive consideration to the interests of agriculture, commerce, industry, services, labor and consumers;
Cannot be officers, directors, employees or stockholders of any bank, or bank, financial or thrift holding company, although a chair must be a person of tested banking experience; and
Must have been residents of the Second Reserve District for two years prior to appointment.

The Class A Directors would interest us the most because they are not only elected by the member banks, but also represent the interests of the member banks(owners). (it's interesting that the class B directors supposedly represent the public, but they also are chosen by the banks....hmmm). Lets look at where the three current Class A directors come from:

CLASS A DIRECTORS

James P. Gorman (2018)
Chairman and Chief Executive Officer
Morgan Stanley

Paul P. Mello (2017)

President and Chief Executive Officer
Solvay Bank

Gerald H. Lipkin (2016)

Chairman, President and Chief Executive Officer
Valley National Bank

We can take from this that, while not a requirement that these directors be from one of the member banks, there is a pretty good chance that they will pick one of their own to represent their interests. So we can conclude that these 3 banks would be member-owners of the New York Fed:

Morgan Stanley

Solvay Bank

Valley National Bank

"Is there a conflict of interest when bankers like JPMorgan Chase CEO Jamie Dimon serve on the board of the same institution that regulates them?Insiders say no. But critics harp on the central bank for what seems like an incestuous relationship with Wall Street." The article also notes "The central bank's most influential branch is undeniably the New York Fed, which sits just blocks away from Wall Street."(5)

So we can add to our list as a member-bank owner:

JPMorgan Chase

While State chartered banks are not required to become member bank (owners) of the New York Fed or any other Fed district, The only list I found while searching The New York Fed's website was a list of state chartered banks that chose to become member-owners:(6)

Second District State Member Banks

Adirondack Bank
Adirondack Trust Company
Alden State Bank
Amboy Bank
Banco Popular De Puerto Rico
Banco Popular North America
Bank of Cattaraugus
Bank of Millbrook
Bank of New York Mellon
BPD Bank
Chemung Canal Trust Company
Community Bank of Bergen County, N.J.
Depository Trust Company
Deutsche Bank Trust Company Americas
Empire State Bank
Five Star Bank
Goldman Sachs Bank USA
Gotham Bank of New York
Manufacturers and Traders Trust Company
Mizuho Corporate Bank (USA)
Northern Trust Company of New York
Orange County Trust Company
Peapack-Gladstone Bank
Solvay Bank
Tioga State Bank
Warehouse Trust Company LLC

Last updated: September, 2012

Some of these being state chartered banks are as we would expect – smaller community type banks. But some conspicuous names are on the list:

Goldman Sachs certainly stands out. As does Bank of New York Mellon, and Northern Trust Co of New York.

The other banks that stand out are some foreign banks (their U.S. subsidiaries, but foreign banks as owners of the New York Fed: Deutsche Bank Trust Company Americas (Germany), Mizuho Corporate Bank (USA) (Japan) and Banco Popular (Spain)

I did more digging – what about going back in time by looking at old annual reports of the New York Fed – where did the previous years Class A directors come from – what banks and institutions did these people represent? This would tell us more member banks, at least on a recent historical level The Class A Directors came from these banks and institutions(7):

2013

Popular, Inc

Valley National Bank

Solvay Bank

2012

JP Morgan Chase & Co

Popular, Inc

Solvay Bank

2011

The Adirondack Trust Company

JP Morgan Chase & Co

Popular, Inc

2010

Popular, Inc

The Adirondack Trust Company

JP Morgan Chase & Co

2009

JP Morgan Chase & Co

Popular, Inc

The Adirondack Trust Company

2008

The Adirondack Trust Company

JP Morgan chase & Co

Popular, inc

2007

The Depository Trust Company

The Adirondack Trust Company

JP Morgan Chase & Co

2006

Citigroup, Inc

The Depository Trust Company

The Adirondack Trust Company

2005

The Adirondack Trust Company

Citigroup, Inc

The Depository Trust Company

2004

The Depository Trust Company

The Adirondack Trust Company

Citigroup, Inc

2003

Citigroup, Inc

The Depository Trust Company

The Adirondack Trust Company

2002

The Canandaigua National Bank and Trust Company

Citigroup, Inc

The Depository Trust Company

2001

FleetBoston Financial

The Canandaigua National Bank and Trust Company

Citigroup, Inc

2000

The Chase Manhattan Corporation

Summit Bancorp

The Canandaigua National Bank and Trust Company

1999

The Canandaigua National Bank and Trust Company

The Chase Manhattan Corporation

Banco Popular de Puerto Rico

1998

Manufacturers and Traders Trust Company, and M&T Bank Corporation (one director CEO of both)

The Canandaigua National Bank and Trust Company

The Chase Manhattan Corporation and The Chase Manhattan Bank (one director CEO of both)

1997

The Bank of New York

Manufacturers and Traders Trust Company, and First Empire State Corporation (one director CEO of both)

The Canandaigua National Bank and Trust Company

1996

Manufacturers and Traders Trust Company

The First National Bank of Long Island

The Bank of New York

1995

Manufacturers and Traders Trust Company

The First National Bank of Long Island

The Bank of New York

Most all the Class A Directors from the Banks and Institutions above were the CEO or Chairman of their respective institution. Of the 20 years of data that we have, some institutions enjoyed representation for a good number of years.

JP Morgan Chase & Co (and predecessors) – 9 years

The Adirondack Trust Company 9 years

Popular, Inc (and predecessors) – 7 years

The Depository Trust Company – 6 years

Why is this important? The Federal Reserve, especially the New York Fed are extremely important to the U.S. money supply. In fact, they control the whole U.S. money supply. So, it's equally important to know who owns and controls them. I'm not saying it's secret, but they seem to go out of their way to conceal the information. They don't just put it out there for all to see.

What we do know is that some of the largest banks in the nation have an ownership stake in the New York Fed – namely JP Morgan Chase & Co, and Citigroup.

The Depository Trust Company is not a publicly traded company – they are owned by their customers – the banks themselves. We don't know which banks own it, and how much they own, and whether any other outside parties of stockholders exist.

Not all the owners of the New York Fed are banks in the true sense of the word. We know that Goldman Sachs as well as Morgan Stanley are owners. These are investment banks that have a direct ownership in the institution that makes the U.S. money. It just screams conflict of interest.

As bad as all this is, perhaps the most unnerving is the fact that there is *some truth* to those old conspiracy theories that foreign banks own and control our nation's central bank. They may or may not "control" the Fed system, but we know that at least 3 foreign banks have ownership shares in the New York Federal Reserve bank. Deutsche Bank Trust Company Americas (Germany), Mizuho Corporate Bank USA (Japan) and Banco Popular (Spain). We know that Popular,Inc has been very active, as their CEO has recently been on the board of directors of the New York Fed. So, they're not just quietly in the shadows – they're actively involved in planning the direction of the U.S. Federal Reserve System.

I was excited to find that a man by the name of Mitchell Langbert had filed a Freedom of Information request to force the Federal Reserve to turn over their list of owners. And it was recent – 2014! Mr Langbert posted the entire list for all the world to see on his blog(20). Unfortunately, it is literally a list of owners and that is it. It does not say anything of ownership percentages or number of shares. It does not even tell you the vital and important info of which particular Federal Reserve bank . It is just a long list of owners – nothing more. (and long it is! 149 pages of just names!). It is obvious to me that the Federal Reserve purposefully made the list in such a way that you can learn little from studying it (after all in 1914, they could devise a precise list of owners divided by each particular district). They purposefully complied with the letter of the law, but not with the spirit of disclosure, that is for sure. We can still learn something from the list, like what foreign banks own a share of our money printing Federal Reserve System as a whole. Some of the more interesting owners that turned up on the list:

Standard Chartered Bank International

Mizuho Bank USA

Banco Pichincha Miami Agency

Banco International De Costa Rica,S.A. Miami Agency

French American Banking Corporation

Petra International Banking Corporation

Banco Santander International

Banco Popular De Puerto Rico

HSBC USA

Mitsubishi UFJ Trust and Banking Corporation

Banco Del Pacifico S.A.

Bank of Tokyo- Mitsubishi UFJ LTD

Bank of Montreal

Royal Bank of Canada

Bank Leumi LE – Israel B.M.

Barclays Bank PLC

Sumitomo Mitsui Banking Corporation

Toronto-Dominion Bank

Mizuho Bank LTD

Bank of Nova Scotia

Israel Discount Bank Limited

Australia and New Zealand Banking Group Limited

National Australia Bank Limited

Banco Do Brasil S.A.

State Bank of India

Bank of East Asia Limited

Malta Banquo, Inc

Banco Bilbao Vizcaya Argentaria, S.A.

UBS AG Tampa Branch Weehawken Loan Production office

Ireland Bancorp, LTD

Some interesting American Firms:

General Electric Capital Corporation

America International Group, Inc

Merrill Lynch International Finance Company

Morgan Financial Corporation

American Express Company

Discover Financial Services

Drexel Morgan and Co.

In researching for the member banks, I came across a historical publication entitled "List Of Member Banks, By Groups In Federal Reserve District No._" and had different sections for each District" It was dated "As Of May 27,1914".(13). This was from the website of the Chicago Fed, but had every district listed, including The New York Fed. If it were a current list, it would be a goldmine of information. At 100 years old, it can still be helpful on a historical level. I rushed immediately to District 2 (New York Fed). Most names on the list are old bank names that mean little to us now. A few names were familiar:

Canandaigua National Bank

Bank Of New York, National Banking Association

Chase National Bank

Gotham National Bank

We know Canandaigua National Bank, and Chase in its latter incarnations have remained very active by supplying board members in recent years. These banks were there at or almost at, the beginning of the system.

Who Really Represents We The People?

In my research, I also uncovered some other interesting and scary facts... The 3 members that are Class A represent the banks and are elected by the banks. The 3 members of the board that are Class B directors are supposed to represent the public, but are not elected by the public. They too are elected by the member banks (the owners of the New York Fed). "...the Federal Reserve banks were (and remain) technically private entities, and private sector banks were given the power to appoint two-thirds of their directors" (9) The banks that own the Federal Reserve Bank Of New York certainly take every bit of this power to their advantage. What a conflict of interest this is – the member bank-owners elect 6 of the 9 members up there on the board. Let's give them the benefit of the doubt for a moment and look at the people they have elected as Class B directors to represent the public over the past 20 years.

The Class B directors that the member bank-owners have elected to the board of the New York Fed to *represent the Public* have included: The CEO of PepsiCo, one of the world's largest food and beverage manufacturers. The CEO of Pfizer, the world's largest pharmaceutical corporation. The CEO of Loews Corporation – a conglomerate with interests in insurance, hotels, and drilling controlled by the Tisch family. The CEO of General Electric, a major industrial and financial corporation. And best of all...the CEO of Lehman Brothers, the investment bank that ultimately went bankrupt in the Great Recession.

I have nothing against any of these CEOs. I don't even blame them for taking the position that the banks offered them. It's not their fault. It's the fault of the system as it's constructed. It's laughable to think that these high powered CEOs "represent the public". I don't feel like the CEO of GE or Pfizer represent "me" – do you feel like they are a good representative of you? All the companies that these CEOs represent have deep banking relationships with the banks, with Wall Street firms, and with investment banks. I don't know how the bankers could even keep a straight face when they elected Richard S. Fuld Jr, the Chairman and CEO of Lehman Brothers in 2004 to serve from 2005 to 2007 to represent "the people". He obviously was "one of their own". It makes a mockery of the whole process. This proves that the Federal Reserve Bank of New York and The Federal Reserve System as a whole is accountable to nobody in practice.

Even President Woodrow Wilson at first refused to sign the Federal Reserve Act into law "because he objected to the provisions for the selection of Class B Directors"(14). President Wilson knew that this was all wrong and would translate into We The People not really being represented at all on the Federal Reserve Board. He changed his mind and signed off on the Act only after one of his largest contributors pressed him to do it, and convinced him it would all be corrected in the future. (It never has been, and it's 2016 now). He signed the Federal Reserve Act on Dec.23,1913. "On that day the Constitution ceased to be the governing covenant of the American people and our liberties were handed over to a small group of international bankers"(14).

Despite all the shenanigans the Fed hasn't even succeeded in their purposes. The panics and collapses continue to happen in the markets. Their defense of the dollar's value has not happened as the dollar has continually declined in purchasing power (Note: banks *do* have an incentive to choose inflation, as this makes the debts of large banks easier to manage). Thomas Piketty's book "Capital – in the Twenty-First Century says "Once currency ceases to be convertible into precious metals, however, the power of central banks to create money is potentially unlimited and must therefore be strictly regulated"(10).

So, were the central banks "strictly regulated" in practice? I don't think so. "When Tim Geithner testified before Congress shortly after becoming treasury secretary, a congressman asked him about the effectiveness of regulation, and he proudly responded, "I have never been a regulator, for better or worse." He did not even understand that part of his job as president of the NY Fed was to regulate some of the nation's largest financial institutions. Indeed, he seemed offended that the congressman asking the question thought that he was a regulator."(11)

"One only needs to reflect on the dramatic decline in the value of the dollar that has taken place since the Fed was established in 1913. The goods and services you could buy for $1.00 in 1913 now cost nearly $21.00. Another way to look at this is from the perspective of the purchasing power of the dollar itself. It has fallen to less than $0.05 of its 1913 value. We might say that the government and its banking cartel have together stolen $0.95 of every dollar as they have pursued a relentlessly inflationary policy".(16)

It was a rotten deal for We The People. Paul Warburg gave a speech to bankers on October 22, 1915 in which he said "...with the United States turned into a creditor nation for all the world, the boundaries of the field that lies open for us are determined only by our power of safe expansion. The scope of our banking future will ultimately be limited by the amount of gold that we can muster as the foundation of our banking and credit structure."(17). At this point, gold and money were still one. If you wanted to print the money, you needed to have the gold. This would change 18 years later when bankers and the Fed were able to convince the government to sever gold from money. This would be a double win for the international bankers – they would not be constrained by gold – they would be able to print paper money as much as they wanted, and second, they would get the gold and be able to keep it all. While We The People trade this utterly worthless Monopoly Money amongst ourselves, they would hold onto all the gold and wouldn't have to share it. (Paul Warburg's son James Warburg, would be involved with this process and curiously wanted to keep the gold standard. Was this his genuine belief or more disinformation? We'll never know)

At the end of the day, it's all our fault. All of us – We The People as voters and our elected representatives in Congress for allowing all of this nonsense to take place. We should all remember that the financial system worked well before 1913 when the Federal Reserve came into existence. What else came into existence in 1913? The Federal Income Tax. Is it just a coincidence that both the Fed and the income tax came about in the same year? I don't think so. My take is that maintaining a central bank like the Fed is expensive. What better mechanism to foot the bill, but to garnish our wages with an income tax.

Since 1913, We The People have been stuck with both the Fed and an Income tax ever since. They have both grown by leaps and bounds. The income tax of 1913 was "sold" to the American people as only a tax on the rich, but over time just became a tax on us all. The Fed has grown ever more complex and gigantic in size and now it has become a big corrupted engine that acts for its own benefit. Maybe 100+ years of letting private banking interests control our nation's money supply is long enough. Maybe it's time We The People consider getting rid of the Federal Reserve.

Chapter 7 - What the Fed Chairmen have said

When talking about the Federal Reserve, it may be instructive to learn what exactly the heads have said and written. The top position at the Fed is the Fed Chairman. It makes a lot of sense to dig deeper and get the views right from the horse's mouth, so to speak. While there is no way to know what is truly in their hearts and minds, we have the next best thing: their actual statements about the issue of gold.

Paul Volcker

Paul Volcker was chairman of the Fed from Aug. 6, 1979 to Aug 11, 1987. How did he feel about gold? This excerpt sums it up pretty well: "When it comes to a hot topic of today's investment world, Mr. Volcker always had a very strong view on gold. "Gold was the enemy to me because that was a speculative vehicle while I was trying to hold the system together. [The speculators] were on the other side." Then and now, the gold price is viewed as the inverse price of the confidence in the system. If gold is high, it usually means something is amiss. In Volcker's time, the high inflation and budget deficits of the 70s propelled gold from a low of $35 before 1970 to a high of $668 in 1980."(5)

It seems pretty clear how he felt. At least Mr. Volcker didn't beat around the bush. No double talk. To him, gold was the enemy. At least we don't have to debate this point. Why? The late 1970's and early 1980's was a period of very high inflation and interest rates. His reasoning is that he was trying to hold "the system together". This implies that gold was a direct threat. The Fed creates currency and sets interest rates. That's what they do. This paper money that they create can be very unstable. This instability was manifesting itself as massive inflation at the time. The gold price went up as people began to realize just how unstable the paper currency was. The increasing confidence in gold really signaled the lack of confidence in the paper money. As paper money was the product of the Fed, this scenario was embarrassing to both the Fed and the government. Paper money is all about perception. Image is everything. And this unraveling made Volcker and the Fed look stupid. If we see it through this lens, then of course Volcker considered gold the enemy. It was causing him great pain.

One last thought is this: Both the Fed and the government have spent considerable effort to convince us all that gold is not money. That gold is a relic. That gold is not important. It's amusing that Volcker gives gold recognition as his "enemy". After all, if gold is your enemy, aren't you revealing its importance? If it is truly an unimportant relic as the Fed and the government claim, then why would you even consider it an enemy? The Fed's own logic doesn't make sense.

Alan Greenspan

On July 20, 2005, Fed Chairman Alan Greenspan made an appearance before The Financial Services Committee. Congressman Ron Paul questioned him:(1)

Congressman Paul: "Even you, in the 1960s, described the paper system as a scheme for confiscation of wealth...Is it not true that the paper system that we work with today is actually a scheme to default on our debt? And is it not true that, for this reason, that's a good argument for people not-eventually, at some day-wanting to buy Treasury bills because they will be paid back with cheaper dollars?...And aligned with this question, I would like to ask something dealing exactly with gold...If paper money-today it seems to be working rather well-but if the paper system doesn't work, when will the time come? What will the signs be that we should reconsider gold?"

Alan Greenspan, Fed Chairman: "Well, you say central banks own gold-or monetary authorities own gold. The United States is a large gold holder. And you have to ask yourself: Why do we hold gold? And the answer is essentially, implicitly, the one you've raised-namely that, over the generations, when fiat money arose and, indeed the type of problems-which I think you correctly identify-of the 1970s, although the implication that that it was some scheme or conspiracy gives it a much more conscious focus than actually, as I recall, it was occurring. It was more inadvertence that created the basic problems. But as I've testified here before to a similar question, central bankers began to realize in the late 1970s how deleterious a factor the inflation was. And, indeed, since the late 70s central bankers generally have behaved as though we were on the gold standard. And, indeed, the extent of liquidity contraction that has occurred as a consequence of the various different efforts on the part of the monetary authorities is a clear indication that we recognize that excess of credit of liquidity creates inflation which, in turn, undermines economic growth. So that the question is: Would there be any advantage, at this particular stage, in going back to the gold standard? And the answer is: I don't think so, because we're acting as though we were there. Would it have been a question at least open in 1971, as you put it? And the answer is yes. Remember, the gold price was $800 an ounce. We were dealing with extraordinary imbalances, interest rates were up sharply, the system looked to be highly unstable and we needed to do something, and we did something. Paul Volcker, as you may recall, in 1979 came into office and put a very severe clamp on the expansion on credit. And that led to a long sequence of events here, which we are benefiting from up to this date. So I think central banking, I believe, has learned the dangers of fiat money and I think as a consequence of that we've behaved as though there are, indeed, real reserves underneath this system."

I find Mr. Greenspan's answer amazing. Mr. Paul is clearly stating that the paper money we use today is a "scheme for confiscation of wealth" and a "scheme to default on our debt" in his question. The head of the Fed does not dispute these points at all. On the contrary, he basically says yes, but it's not done intentionally. The Fed chairman goes a step further by asking himself "why do we hold gold?" He goes on to answer the question himself, explaining that we hold gold "the one you've raised-namely that, over the generations, when fiat money arose... that created the basic problems". I don't know if the Fed chairman was feeling especially honest this day (It is noted that this was Mr. Greenspan's last appearance before the Financial Services Committee"(1)

Mr. Greenspan goes on with his long answer basically saying how we know that inflation is a danger. Mr. Greenspan says that the reason we don't need to go back to the gold standard is that the Fed is acting as if it were on the gold standard anyway. This *could* be a logical argument. If the Fed really showed serious restraint in printing more money, in *theory*, things could work out OK. The problem is that the world doesn't work that way. When he made this statement, in 2005, the economy was doing alright. In only a few short years, the reality of living in the real world would strike a glancing blow to the theoretical world. With the onset of mortgage meltdowns, troubled assets on bank's balance sheets, and the Great Recession, problems arouse. These problems exerted a force upon the Fed to do something. The forces were both economic and political. Mr. Greenspan had retired when the mess came, but I don't think it would have mattered. My thought is that the pressure on the Fed to print and inject massive amounts of new money into the system was too great for any person to withstand, no matter what their philosophy was.

What is most unusual about Alan Greenspan's exchange with Rep. Paul is the fact that Greenspan was indeed a great believer in gold. This is what Rep Paul is referencing when he speaks of what Greenspan referenced back in the 1960's. It is important to take a look at what Greenspan had written. One example is a paper he published back in 1966 titled "Gold and Economic Freedom". Here is an excerpt of what Greenspan had to say:

"An almost hysterical antagonism toward the gold standard is one issue which unites statists of all persuasions. They seem to sense — perhaps more clearly and subtly than many consistent defenders of laissez-faire — that gold and economic freedom are inseparable, that the gold standard is an instrument of laissez-faire and that each implies and requires the other...the opposition to the gold standard in any form — from a growing number of welfare-state advocates — was prompted by a much subtler insight: the realization that the gold standard is incompatible with chronic deficit spending (the hallmark of the welfare state). Stripped of its academic jargon, the welfare state is nothing more than a mechanism by which governments confiscate the wealth of the productive members of a society to support a wide variety of welfare schemes. A substantial part of the confiscation is effected by taxation. But the welfare statists were quick to recognize that if they wished to retain political power, the amount of taxation had to be limited and they had to resort to programs of massive deficit spending, i.e., they had to borrow money, by issuing government bonds, to finance welfare expenditures on a large scale...In the absence of the gold standard, there is no way to protect savings from confiscation through inflation. There is no safe store of value. If there were, the government would have to make its holding illegal, as was done in the case of gold. If everyone decided, for example, to convert all his bank deposits to silver or copper or any other good, and thereafter declined to accept checks as payment for goods, bank deposits would lose their purchasing power and government-created bank credit would be worthless as a claim on goods. The financial policy of the welfare state requires that there be no way for the owners of wealth to protect themselves. This is the shabby secret of the welfare statists' tirades against gold. Deficit spending is simply a scheme for the confiscation of wealth. Gold stands in the way of this insidious process. It stands as a protector of property rights. If one grasps this, one has no difficulty in understanding the statists' antagonism toward the gold standard."(4)

Mr. Greenspan obviously recognized that gold was a central part of sound money. Not only did he recognize it back then, but he felt the need to broadcast to the world how he felt about it. He laid out some very important points. The most broad is his statement that gold *is* economic freedom. This implies that a world not based on gold has no economic freedom. The world of today has no gold backing any of the world's currencies. Under Greenspan's definition, We The People do *not* have economic freedom.

Mr. Greenspan also lays out his argument that there was political pressure to force productive and working people to shoulder the burden of providing for the welfare recipients. The only way to accomplish this was to take from one group (the productive) and hand it to the welfare class. Taxes would have accomplished this, but Greenspan correctly makes the case that you can only tax to a point. The only way then is to confiscate wealth, and gold was standing in the way. Looking back on this, it makes perfect sense that gold needed to be removed from the monetary system. When Greenspan wrote this paper in 1966, the western world was still on the gold standard because the U.S. dollar was on the gold standard. Those dollars were in the hands of many nations because the dollar was the reserve currency of the world.

As the years wore on, Alan Greenspan climbed the ranks until ultimately he became the chairman of the Fed from 1987 to 2006. Why did Greenspan soften his stance on gold? For one thing, by the time he became the head of the Fed, the dollar had been severed from gold for 16 years already. He could only make do with a system he inherited. This leads to the second and larger issue. – Greenspan had now become the establishment. What was he going to do – speak out against the banking cartel that owns the Fed? Speak out against the government for ending the gold standard in 1971? If he did, even as Fed Chairman, what good would it have done? It surely would have made headlines. But in all likelihood, the banking cartel would not have let him get away with this. One way or another, they would have found a way to remove him. Human nature is what it is. People have the predisposition to take the easiest path forward...in this case, that meant enjoying the privilege and power that came with his chairmanship post.

Ben Bernanke

The Federal Reserve chairman who succeeded Mr. Greenspan was Ben Bernanke. Mr. Bernanke authored a book entitled The Courage To Act – A Memoir Of A Crisis And Its Aftermath. In his book, he shares ideas on his way of thinking. Big banks always choose inflation. This offers them an easy way to service their debts. In his book, Mr. Bernanke shares his views on deflation. In the context of theories on the cause of the Great Depression of the early 1930s "...The Holy Grail of macroeconomics , I would call it-was why the Depression happened, and why it was so long and deep...The sharp decline in the money supply hurt the economy primarily by inducing a severe deflation (falling wages and prices). Prices in the United States fell by nearly 10 percent per year in 1931 and 1932. This violent deflation in turn led households and farms to postpone purchases and capital investments in anticipation of lower prices later, depressing demand and output. Moreover, the international gold standard, which created a monetary link among countries tied to gold, spread America's deflation and depression abroad."(2) He also states in regards to the overheated stock market and crash of 1929 to the Great Depression "(in a tragic sense, the Fed succeeded in its effort to cool the market) but also a too-tight monetary policy that helped cause the Depression"(3). He also says of modern times that "I said that central banks should do whatever they could to avoid deflation. For example, they can set a goal for inflation above zero to provide a buffer, or safety zone, against deflation. Advanced-economy central banks generally aimed for inflation of about 2 percent rather than zero, though in the Fed's case the goal wasn't stated explicitly. I also argued that it was important to get ahead of deflation by cutting rates preemptively if necessary"(3)

From reading Mr Bernanke's remarks, deflation seems like the boogeyman. The word itself sounds scary. But really all it means is the money is strengthening. Your money will buy you more and more as time goes by. Historically, during the Great Depression the economy was going to hell. Everything was a mess. Money back in those days was real money – it was gold coin. So your gold (the money) was experiencing more and more demand from We The People that wanted it. Because of this dynamic, the price of goods in relation to your gold (money) was falling. This is a good thing for savers. Their prudence and conservatism are rewarded and vindicated.

Mr. Bernanke was an inflationist, as all central bankers are. I think he is trying to justify his inflationary mind set and record of printing hundreds of billions of dollars out of thin air. Mr. Bernanke makes the argument that this is the aim of every central banker – to always add some inflation to the system. It is a dangerous argument because what he is really saying is your money should decline in value by 2% per year. Under this monetary system goal, you would be foolish to want to save money at all – it becomes an eroding financial asset rather than a growing or even stable one. It is a major disincentive to saving money. It hurts the fiscally conservative and prudent in society, and benefits the reckless that have too much debt (like most of the big banks). It is ultimately a system of wealth redistribution carried out by the Fed. Gold stood in the way of these wicked ideas and plans. It had to be eliminated, and that is exactly what happened in 1933 for We The People.

Chapter 8 - 1933 –gold is confiscated

On April 5 1933 President Franklin D. Roosevelt issued executive order 6102. This order effectively required U.S. citizens to turn over their gold coins and bullion and even their gold certificates. In doing so, President Roosevelt violated two different laws.

First, the president violated the United States Constitution. In the constitution Article 1 Section 10 Clause 1 states "No State shall enter into any Treaty, Alliance, or Confederation; grant Letters of Marque and Reprisal; coin Money; emit Bills of Credit; make any Thing but Gold and Silver Coin a Tender in Payment of Debts; pass any Bill of Attainder, ex post facto Law, or Law impairing the Obligation of Contracts, or grant any Title of Nobility."

Some claim that this argument is not valid because while the Constitution does make clear that gold and silver must be used, it is referencing the states and the states only and thus the federal government is exempt. The problem for those arguing this point of logic is that back when this was written into the Constitution, the states were the ones coining money in the U.S. As unbelievable as it sounds, the federal government did not get into the coining of money until years later. People back in those early days gave much more power to the states than to the federal government as they did not trust a strong central government. All things considered it seems pretty clear what the intent of the Constitution says. It pretty plainly spells out that silver and gold were to be the coinage of the land. To try and get around this by using a technicality of the Clause not mentioning the federal government is therefore a pretty weak argument considering that the feds didn't coin back then. It would have actually been strange if it *was* mentioned explicitly.

Second, President Roosevelt violated the purview of the U.S. Congress. Article 1, Section 8, Clause 5 of the United States Constitution states "The Congress shall have Power to...coin Money, regulate the Value thereof, and of foreign Coin..." This seems to certainly make it clear that dealing with the nation's money is the scope of the Congress. It says nothing of a president dealing in such matters. In this clause we see a couple of interesting tidbits of information. First, that congress seems to be implying that eventually the nation will coin the money and not just leave it up to the states indefinitely. Second, I find it to be even more telling that it states to "coin Money". Notice how coin and money are linked together here in this clause . It does not mention paper money at all. During the revolutionary war, continental currency was the "money" used out of necessity, so the Congress clearly had knowledge of what paper money was – more than likely these men used paper themselves in the past to make transactions. Yet no mention is made of it. I don't think this is a coincidence. They surely remember what a disaster this paper currency turned into and wanted no part of it.

So in this context the president violated the Constitution again as well as violated the power that was exclusive to the Congress. Congress was and is closer to the people as the members come from specific regions of the country. They are more answerable to the people in this regard. Even today the phrase "your man in Congress" is used because these individuals are supposed to represent us from our local area on the national stage and be more in tune to how We The People feel. This is why the congressman has only a 2 year term today – to keep them accountable to the people they represent. No wonder people felt a little more comfort giving Congress this awesome power as opposed to the president or court system. Lastly, the president violated what money is – the very definition of money by abandoning gold in the domestic market.

People sometimes get confused when they realize there was paper money circulating back then. But the paper back then was different than the paper we use now. There were Silver Certificates or Gold Certificates. Gold Certificates were the larger denomination paper currency of the day. When you look at one of these Gold Certificates, it clearly spells out exactly what is being represented by it. For example when you look at a $20 bill from the series of 1928, at first glance it looks very much like the modern $20 bill we use today with a couple of important exceptions. The first difference and most obvious is the seal and serial numbers are gold in color and says "GOLD CERTIFICATE" on the note. The second and more important difference is under the portrait of Andrew Jackson It says "TWENTY DOLLARS" much like modern notes but under that it reads "IN GOLD COIN PAYABLE TO THE BEARER ON DEMAND". So really what this is saying is that the $20 bill was the same as having a $20 Gold coin (called a "Double Eagle"). The paper currency of the day was just a convenience so you wouldn't have to lug around the physical gold coins. They were a claim check on the gold coin, and thus treated the same.

So the paper money served as a basic contract between the U.S. government and the citizens. This is why the government needed to also get their hands on as many of the Gold Certificates as they possibly could.

When you go back on your word, you don't want all these contracts out there to remind people of how you had promised that this piece of paper was as good as the physical gold.

Why didn't people scoff at giving up their gold back in 1933? It should be remembered that in the early 1930's the country was in the thick of the Great Depression. The simple answer is that the majority of people simply did not have gold coins or Gold Certificates or bullion in any significant quantity– they were simply scraping by in their lives, living paycheck to paycheck. The average annual salary for 1932 -1934 was only $1,368. Some examples of annual salaries: Steel worker $423, public school teacher: $1,227, hired farm hand: $216, Doctor: $3,382, bus driver $1,373, secretary $1,040. Living expenses were also lower. Men's shoes were an average of $4. Men's suit $10.50, bicycle $7. A night at the Waldorf Astoria in New York City could be had for $5 to $10 per night.(1)

The wages were not high, but neither were the costs of living. The real problem was actually having a job that paid *anything*. The Department of Labor states that "the Bureau of Labor Statistics later estimated that 12,830,000 persons were out of work in 1933, about one-fourth of a civilian labor force of over fifty-one million. March was the record month, with about fifteen and a half million unemployed. There is no doubt that 1933 was the worst year, and March the worst month for joblessness in the history of the United States."(2) With the unemployment rate at a whopping 25% (over 30% in March!) people were desperate for some changes. These were the times in our country that saw bread lines snaking around city blocks. It must have felt like the world was ending for these millions of people without work. They would be easy pickings for someone that wanted to get elected by promising sweeping changes. It's hard to stand on principle when you are starving.

The wealthy did have gold. But even those who would have wanted to fight the government for their constitutional rights were faced with a daunting threat. The order threatened a severe $10,000 fine and/or a 10 year prison sentence for failing to comply. Evidently, the government really wanted the gold and wasn't above using mafia - like threats and tactics to accomplish their goals. This explains why when you research this topic you don't find much evidence of overt resistance by people. There was an exemption for "rare and unusual" coins up to $100 aimed at collectors, but this was not defined and nobody at the time really knew what that meant. Many people must have thought it too nebulous to take the risk of fines and prison – what if the government declared what you were keeping was not rare or unusual enough?

That's not to say that nobody fought. One man in particular named Frederick Barber Campbell dared to defy the government. The story is rather remarkable because it was one of the few instances where someone took action against this injustice. Mr. Campbell was a wealthy elderly man who was a lawyer in New York City. He had chosen the Chase National Bank to be the custodian of his gold. On two separate occasions, he brought gold bars for the bank to hold for him (around 5000 plus ounces!). In September of 1933 the bank notified Mr. Campbell that it was required to surrender his gold bullion to the government, citing the president's executive order. Three days later Mr. Campbell demanded his gold back from the bank. The bank refused. Mr. Campbell sued Chase for his gold back. The next day, Mr. Campbell was indicted for failing to register and turn over his gold. The prosecution of Mr. Campbell was not successful. The government lost in the sense that it was found that the legalese the president used was not really correct and this actually forced the government to reissue the executive order with the treasurer signing off on this. Mr. Campbell did eventually lose his gold to the government. There was talk about launching an appeal to the Supreme Court back then, but it never happened. This is too bad, because one has to wonder what would have happened if the highest court ruled in his favor. We'll never know. The gold confiscation became "legal" and "OK" really on the basis of nobody challenging it all the way. We can't blame old Mr. Campbell here – he certainly did his part to fight the good fight on behalf of liberty and with a huge fine and 10 year prison term looming over him, who can blame him for not wanting any more of the court proceedings.

To be fair, many people did turn in their gold holdings. The information below from Numismaster(4) shows how many coins were taken in:

Gold coins melted by the Mint

	$1 gold	$2.50 Gold	$3 Gold	$5 gold	$10 gold	$20 gold
Total Minted	19.8748	20.4268	0.5398	78.9119	57.6835	174.1056
Total Melted	0.0319	3.2049	0.0583	26.5723	27.1974	67.9063
Remaining	19.8429	17.2220	0.4815	52.3395	30.4861	106.1994
Melted% of Minted	0.16%	15.69%	10.80%	33.67%	47.15%	39.00%
%Remaining	99.84%	84.31%	89.20%	66.33%	52.85%	61.00%
BY YEAR:						
1933	3,128	1,585,851	284	6,945,392	7,772,007	39,245,317
1934	4,423	737,468	1,272	8,770,390	7,526,849	23,638,308
1935	455	8,687	41	161,414	2,200,892	3,355,580
1936	717	13,500	69	31,856	19,721	71,394
1937	464	11,090	52	21,144	11,741	25,175
1938	533	13,900	62	30,974	18,239	32,804
1939	323	29	751	17,711	10,998	14,866
TOTAL 1933-39	10,043	2,370,524	2,531	15,978,881	17,560,446	66,383,444
Total 1867-1950	31,862	3,204,854	58,304	26,572,327	27,197,378	67,906,256
Recall % of all total	31.52%	73.97%	4.34%	60.13%	64.57%	97.76%

When reviewing this information, we can see that the government kept meticulous records of the exact numbers of coins by type that were taken in and melted (unfortunately for collectors of coins the mint did not record the coin's year and mint mark so this will never be known, and by extension it will never be known how many coins survive of a particular year and mint mark to determine a coin's rarity). We can see from the information above that 1933 saw the most $20 and $10 gold coins melted followed closely by 1934. The $20 gold coin has a staggeringly high number of coins melted – over 39 million in 1933 alone and over 23 million in 1934. This is somewhat to be expected as when you look at the mintage figure for the $20 gold coin there were over 174 million produced over the years....why so many? The $20 gold coin in particular was used mainly by the banks as part of their reserves. We must remember that $20 was a huge sum of money in the 19th and early 20th century. Regular folks didn't usually walk around with that much money. It would be like someone today carrying around a $1,000 bill (if they were still in print) in their wallet or purse. Some people may carry that much currency, but not many.

The rich of course had this gold but the population basically said "screw the rich". As is usually the case when the masses want to screw the rich, what happens is they end up screwing themselves and the rich find ways around the rules. This is exactly what took place back in 1933.

Many people that had gold simply sent their gold holdings to European banks for safe keeping, where it remained their property but outside of the U.S. confiscation law. There is no hard data on how many of these coins were sent over but we now know it was significant enough that even to this day, coin dealers run advertisements in coin collector's magazines boasting they receive fresh deliveries from Europe monthly. Even though a massive amount of coins were taken in and melted down by the government, if we look at the math of mintage minus melted we can see many survived. They either survived by heading to safe haven banks in Europe or by staying in the United States by people deciding to risk it by holding them in violation of federal law.

The general public should have known better. They had been through this before just 20 years earlier with income taxes. There was no regular federal income tax in the United States until 1913. How do you sell people on paying part of your hard earned income to the government? Did they praise the virtues of being patriotic in 1913 to help pay for government operations? No. In 1913 the people went along with a federal income tax because it only applied to the rich. The population basically said – "yeah, screw the rich, make them pay". The problem is that once the government got a taste of this money, they were addicted until the definition of "rich" was repeatedly lowered to include more and more people who found they must also pay. Today nearly everyone has to pay federal income taxes, even the working poor making minimum wage. By trying to screw the rich We The People now find ourselves with a system that forces secretaries to pay a higher percentage of their income than their billionaire bosses, because the rich have all these loopholes the average citizen does not.

So how did this gold confiscation turn out? The government got its gold which it paid $20.67 per ounce of gold. The price of gold was then raised by the government to $35 an ounce. "The cost of an ounce of gold had climbed from $20.67 to $35, a hike of almost 70 percent.

It had happened very fast, and for one reason – the United States had been cooking the price."(3). What a neat trick the government had managed to pull off for itself! It bought gold on the cheap by forcing law abiding citizens into selling, and then had a nearly 70% upside profit it could use in foreign governmental transactions! The rub of course that this "free" wealth the federal government engineered for itself wasn't free at all – it was *stolen* from the American people – to the tune of almost 70% of the value. If this was done by a private business, this would be called something: Robbery!

Chapter 9 – 1971 – The Dollar Becomes a Complete Fiction

1971 was a pivotal year because this is when the U.S. Dollar was officially de-linked to gold. To gain an understanding of how and why this came to be, we need to examine the system in which the dollar and gold were operating on at the time and the years leading up to 1971. The system was called the Bretton Woods System.

The system was named after the town of Bretton Woods, NH, where a meeting took place in 1944, as World War 2 was nearing an end. This meeting was "...attended by representatives of the forty-four major allied world powers. The United States was one of the few economies that had not had its infrastructure destroyed through bombing, and its output now represented over half of the global economy. This put U.S. negotiators in an excellent position to encourage the rest of the world to accept the U.S. dollar as the world's de facto reserve currency...All other currencies were fixed to the U.S. dollar, which was redeemable in gold by foreign holders at $35 an ounce. This was not the 1:1 ratio that existed under the "classical gold standard" but rather a "gold exchange standard" whereby, for every $100 in circulation, $40 worth of gold was held in a vault backing it. The dollar was therefore 40 percent backed by gold...The problem with this system was that there was no restriction on how many dollars the Federal Reserve could produce...The Fed continued to create currency ...(the U.S. government) attempting to fight the Vietnam War while introducing expensive new Social Security improvements, the peg to gold became more difficult to maintain...The combined expenses stretched the dollar's relationship to the point that there was no longer enough gold to back it. This caused foreign governments to become increasingly suspicious and, subsequently, they began redeeming their dollars for gold. Leading this campaign was President Charles de Gaulle of France, who began redeeming U.S. dollars for gold at such an unsustainable rate that it eventually led to Nixon's breaking of the peg."(1)

Why did the other nations allow the U.S. to take such a lead? Was it just because the infrastructure of our country was still intact? There is an old saying that seems relevant here...it goes something like this: "Remember the golden rule. Those who have the gold make the rules". The United States had the most gold. "...the US had 60 per cent of the world's bullion. Instead of tying currencies to gold, they were tied to the dollar."(4)

On the surface, President Nixon gets the blame for breaking the tie of the U.S. dollar to gold backing. In reality, The Federal Reserve was to blame for its overprinting of the currency. President Nixon was basically backed into a corner. If he allowed the U.S. dollar to keep its gold peg, then foreign nations would over time continue to take gold out of our country and our nation's gold supply would have been wiped out. He knew that the American people would not give him too much flack on this because their rights to trade dollars for gold was long gone...that right had disappeared in 1933. In fact, in 1971, it was still illegal for Americans to even own gold bullion with the exception of a handful of old "collector coins".

In reality, we can see that in 1971, the U.S. dollar was backed by gold more in theory rather than in reality. It may have comforted people to know that the dollar was "backed by gold" when they looked at their paper money. But this was at best only quasi true. The backing only applied to foreign nations holding U.S. dollars, and even then it wasn't a 100% backing.

President Nixon did what he had to do. He had to close the "gold window" that allowed foreign nations to keep exchanging their paper dollars for American gold. Unfortunately, by doing this, he turned U.S. paper money into pure fiat money...money that had no backing whatsoever. The U.S. government still has large gold reserves, but they do not back our currency. The U.S. paper money from 1971 to today became just a fancy looking Monopoly Money that we all use. "In 1971 President Nixon abandoned the obligation for the US Federal Reserve to exchange dollars for gold at a set rate. At that time, gold was valued at just $35 a troy ounce; by August 2011, it was trading at $1,900 an ounce. That shift illustrates what those who believed in sound money feared would happen – paper money has an inherent tendency to lose its value. Some would say it is bound to decline to its intrinsic value: zero. In the critics' view, paper money is about as solid as air miles; the kind of currency that you accumulate but can never really cash in."(2)

Gold, from 1971 to today, has been a competitor to the dollar, and the government has been trying to convince everyone of how gold is irrelevant ever since. It became the anti-dollar. If you're buying and holding gold, you are basically going short on the dollar – in other words, if your betting on gold increasing, then what you are really doing, is betting on a decline of the dollar. Over the past decades, this has been a pretty good bet. Some back in 1971 thought that by eliminating the dollar's peg with gold, that gold would be hurt and its price plummet. These folks got it all wrong – the gold was holding up the value of the dollar, not the other way around. The dollar plummeted in value, gold would skyrocket in value.

Looking back on what happened in 1971, I think President Nixon missed a golden opportunity to right some old mistakes. Instead of just eliminating the peg to gold for foreign nations, he could have went one step further, and restored the ability of American citizens to convert their dollars to gold. Instead of telling no to the foreign nations and leaving the dollars as Monopoly Money, he could have accomplished something historic. The dollar was technically already on the gold standard. He could have just flipped the right to redeem dollars for gold to We The People *only*. If the argument was that there was not enough gold to do this, then a new backing of say 10% or 5% could have been used instead of the 40% backing. He could have reversed the unconstitutional executive order that President Roosevelt had perpetrated in 1933. Even a smaller partial backing would have preserved some integrity to dollars.

As it worked out, President Nixon didn't even reverse the laws that made it illegal for Americans to invest in bullion gold. That honor belongs to his successor, President Ford. "From 1933 to 1974, private gold ownership was a touchy subject for Americans. An executive order issued by President Franklin D. Roosevelt in 1933 criminalized the hoarding of gold, though numismatic gold coins were generally exempt from the law. Public Law 93-373, signed by President Ford on Dec.31, 1974, brought an end to the ban that prevented U.S. citizens from freely owning gold. A new "gold rush" of sorts occurred on Jan.1, 1975, when U.S. coin collectors, gold bugs, and metal investors were free to purchase the yellow metal in coin and bullion form for the first time in two generations ."(3)

Chapter 10 - Bank for International Settlements (BIS) – The most powerful bank you've never heard of

The Bank for International Settlements (or "BIS" as it is commonly referred to) is the central banker's bank. It serves and is owned by its member banks, who are the central banks of the world. It came into existence in 1930, originally as a way of dealing with the reparations that Germany had to pay to the Allies after World War One. It is headquartered in Basel, Switzerland.

The BIS was granted extraordinary power and protection from the beginning. "The Swiss authorities have no jurisdiction over the BIS premises. Founded by an international treaty, and further protected by the 1987 Headquarters Agreement with the Swiss government, the BIS enjoys similar protections to those granted to the headquarters of the United Nations, the International Monetary Fund (IMF) and diplomatic embassies. The Swiss authorities need the permission of the BIS management to enter the bank's buildings, which are described as "Inviolable". The BIS has the right to communicate in code and to send and receive correspondence in bags covered by the same protection as embassies, meaning they cannot be opened. The BIS is exempt from Swiss taxes. Its employees do not have to pay income tax on their salaries....The bank's extraordinary legal privileges also extend to its staff and directors. Senior managers enjoy special status, similar to that of diplomats, while carrying out their duties in Switzerland, which means their bags cannot be searched (unless there is evidence of a blatant criminal act), and their papers are inviolable. The central bank governors traveling to Basel for the bimonthly meetings enjoy the same status while in Switzerland. All bank officials are immune under Swiss law, for life, for all the acts carried out during the discharge of their duties."(1)

The BIS is definitely not anything like your friendly neighborhood bank. "The Bank's capital is held by central banks only. Sixty central banks and monetary authorities are currently members of the BIS and have rights of voting and representation at General Meetings(3)

Bank of Algeria

Central Bank of Argentina

Reserve Bank of Australia

Central Bank of the Republic of Austria

National Bank of Belgium

Central Bank of Bosnia and Herzegovina

Central Bank of Brazil

Bulgarian National Bank

Bank of Canada

Central Bank of Chile

People's Bank of China

Bank of the Republic (Colombia)

Croatian National Bank

Czech National Bank

Danmarks Nationalbank (Denmark)

Bank of Estonia

European Central Bank

Bank of Finland

Bank of France

Deutsche Bundesbank (Germany)

Bank of Greece

Hong Kong Monetary Authority

Magyar Nemzeti Bank (Hungary)

Central Bank of Iceland

Reserve Bank of India

Bank Indonesia

Central Bank of Ireland

Bank of Israel

Bank of Italy

Bank of Japan

Bank of Korea

Bank of Latvia

Bank of Lithuania

Central Bank of Luxembourg

National Bank of the Republic of Macedonia

Central Bank of Malaysia

Bank of Mexico

Netherlands Bank

Reserve Bank of New Zealand

Central Bank of Norway

Central Reserve Bank of Peru

Bangko Sentral ng Pilipinas (Philippines)

National Bank of Poland

Bank of Portugal

National Bank of Romania

Central Bank of the Russian Federation

Saudi Arabian Monetary Agency

National Bank of Serbia

Monetary Authority of Singapore

National Bank of Slovakia

Bank of Slovenia

South African Reserve Bank

Bank of Spain

Sveriges Riksbank (Sweden)

Swiss National Bank

Bank of Thailand

Central Bank of the Republic of Turkey

Central Bank of the United Arab Emirates

Bank of England

Board of Governors of the Federal Reserve System (United States)

Its board is made up of the most powerful financial heads in the world. "The Board of Directors may have up to 21 members, including six ex officio directors, comprising the central bank Governors of Belgium, France, Germany, Italy, the United Kingdom and the United States. Each ex officio member may appoint another member of the same nationality. Nine Governors of other member central banks may be elected to the Board."(2) The current list of board members are(2)

Chairman: Jens Weidmann, Frankfurt am Main
Vice-Chairman: Raghuram G Rajan, Mumbai

Mark Carney, London
Agustín Carstens, Mexico City
Luc Coene, Brussels
Jon Cunliffe, London
Mario Draghi, Frankfurt am Main
William C Dudley, New York
Stefan Ingves, Stockholm
Thomas Jordan, Zurich
Klaas Knot, Amsterdam
Haruhiko Kuroda, Tokyo
Anne Le Lorier, Paris
Fabio Panetta, Rome
Stephen S Poloz, Ottawa
Jan Smets, Brussels
Alexandre A Tombini, Brasília
François Villeroy de Galhau, Paris

Ignazio Visco, Rome
Janet L Yellen, Washington
Zhou Xiaochuan, Beijing

While these people may not be household names, they represent the biggest and strongest central banks in the world. For example, Janet Yellen is the head of the Federal Reserve (she took over when Ben Bernanke retired). The others on the list are the heads of the central banks of their countries.

We know that the BIS certainly likes gold. As of Febuary, 2015, the BIS is number 33 on the list of the largest gold holdings in the world with ownership of 111 Tonnes of gold(4). It is further noted that the "BIS data are updated each year from the BIS's annual report to reflect the Bank's gold investment assets excluding any gold held in connection with swap operations, under which the Bank exchanges currencies for physical gold. The bank has an obligation to return the gold at the end of the contract"(4). The amount of gold owned would be expected to fluctuate, as this is essentially the bank's business model. "The gold standard is long gone, but...it is certainly ever more central to the BIS's banking operations, so much so that the Financial Times has described the bank as "the ultimate bullion pawnbroker". ..meaning that the bank exchanges currencies for gold, which it returns at the end of the contract"(5)

Needless to say, the BIS is an enormously powerful institution. How has it used its power? Has it used it to "do the right thing" for humanity? No. Not really. Most people don't consider collaborating with the Nazis as doing the right thing. We are reminded that the BIS is a bank, and like any bank, it seeks to maximize doing what is right for its bottom line. Profit comes first, everything else comes second.

The BIS had disturbingly close ties to Nazi Germany. An American by the name of Thomas McKittrick was actually president of the BIS from 1940 to 1946. The fact that an American was the leader of the BIS during the entire World War 2 period makes it seem unbelievable how the BIS conducted itself immediately before and during the war. "...many of the things that McKittrick was doing, such as gold and foreign exchange deals with the Reichsbank after Pearl Harbor, were treasonable".(10)

Even before taking his post as president of the BIS in January 1940, McKittrick went to "help Hitler's former propaganda chief get released from a British prison camp. In October 1939 Ernst Hanfstaengel's lawyers asked McKittrick to provide a character reference for their client...one of Hitler's earliest backers. ..his eccentric mannerisms, dry sense of humor, and close connection to Hitler made him enemies, and he fled in 1937"(7) . With McKittrick's help, he did get released.

"Until 1942, the BIS could buy and sell gold at better rates than the Swiss National Bank. This Bizarre setup, where Allied and Axis bankers worked together so profitably, drew increasingly hostile attention in London and Washington,DC. The State department asked the American Embassy in London to investigate the state of the relationship between the British government and the BIS...John Gilbert Winant, the ambassador, met with Sir Otto Niemeyer, the former chairman of the BIS board. Niemeyer was as adamant as ever about the BIS's immunity. He pointed to article 10 of the BIS's charter that guaranteed that in the event of war, the property and assets of the bank shall be immune from seizure."(8). It is clear from this exchange that the BIS was going to flex its muscles and endeavor to use all its special privileges to its advantage.

Some American leaders in government were taking notice of this cozy and intertwined relationship that the BIS and the Swiss had with Nazi Germany. "The Treasury Department did not share the State Department's enthusiasm for McKittrick and the BIS. Henry Morgenthau, the Treasury secretary, and his colleague, Harry Dexter White, loathed the BIS, seeing it, correctly, as a channel for the perpetuation of Nazi economic interests in the United States. They ensured that the bank was facing ever more obstacles to doing business in the United States...The Treasury Department believed that Swiss banks were being used to transfer ownership of Italian and German firms to Swiss or American front companies. Their investigators were unraveling the links between New York, Berlin, and Bern. For example, Felix Islelin, a Swiss banker, was the chairman of IG Chemie, the Swiss subsidiary of IG Farben, the industrial conglomerate that drove the Nazi war machine and whose chairman, Hermann Schmitz, sat on the BIS board. Iselin also sat on the board of the Swiss Bank Corporation and the Credit Suisse bank. IG Chemie was a holding company for General Aniline and Film, IG Farben's American subsidiary."(9). When we consider IG Farben's role in Nazi Germany- everything from using slave labor at the concentration camps to actually making the Zyklon B gas used in the gas chambers, we can see the trouble of having its head sit on the board of the BIS, helping direct policy.

"Germany was also shipping gold to the BIS, McKittrick explained, : "You see we had a lot of German investments, which were made in '31 in accordance with the statutes of the bank. We had to help Germany with loans to pay for reparations payments in the first years...they had to pay us about a million Swiss Francs a month and that is what we lived on. And in order to give us that money they would ship gold to us. Now, we had no vaults. We had no place to handle gold. We had none of the necessary devices to assay gold or weigh gold. They (the SNB) have a scale as big as that chimney breast there, and you can weigh the weight of your signature on a piece of paper. So we had the Bank of Switzerland do all our gold handling and gold storing for us in Switzerland."(11)

An intelligence source cabled American officials dated June 23,1943 and said "German gold shipments (gold bars) arriving here, which were referred to recently, seem to be for the account of the Bank for International Settlements. The value involved is small, approximately Swiss Francs 750,000 at a time. The gold, upon the arrival at the National Bank of Switzerland, Bern, is passed to the credit of the Basel bank"(13)

"The BIS also held gold for the Reichsbank so sometimes, when interest was due on the bank's investments, the BIS simply helped itself to the Nazi gold it held to make up the payments, McKittrick explained. At other times, the Germans borrowed BIS gold for their dealings with Swiss banks. This cozy arrangement caused no concern at the BIS, said McKittrick as "we knew that they'd replace it."(13) I find these couple of sentences to be the most damning of both McKittrick and the BIS itself. The BIS would just help itself to some of the Nazi gold...did they ever even stop to think about exactly where this gold was coming from? It was bad enough that the Germans were sending gold to the BIS, but how was that gold obtained?

"The SS was a business as well as a killing machine, the state engine of looting, plunder, and despoliation, from the gold extracted from the teeth of concentration camp victims to the banks, steelworks, factories, and chemical plants of Nazi-occupied countries"(14). The SS was the trusted "elite" that Hitler trusted to run the concentration camps, gas chambers, and do all the gruesome work that had to be done. Hitler's own guards – the soldiers around him, charged with his protection – those were SS troops, not the regular army. The SS basically plundered anything of value they could get their hands on.

The BIS was therefore engaged in gold laundering for Nazi Germany. This was literally 'blood money" or more accurately "blood gold". From the very admission of the president of the BIS, did they stop to ask any questions? Think about the morals of what they were accepting? I don't think they did. And the notion that they "didn't know" doesn't really hold up – then as now, the people running the BIS are extremely powerful people with a vast network of government contacts all around the world. They most likely would have heard rumors, at the least. It was a fact that Nazi Germany was conquering most of Europe, so at the least, they would have known that some of the gold was stolen property. By the president of the BIS' own statement, they helped themselves to some of the gold. I think they were all too happy to do this, and didn't care a thing about the people, the war, or anything else.

What became of Mr. McKittrick after the war? Was he ever prosecuted or thrown in prison? No – he got a sort of promotion. "Thomas McKittrick had a lucrative new job. Soon after he stepped down as BIS president in 1946, he was appointed a Vice President of Chase

National Bank in New York, in charge of foreign loans. McKittrick was even lauded by those whose stolen goods he had purveyed. He was invited to Brussels and decorated with the Royal Order of the Crown of Belgium. The honor, noted a press release, was "in recognition of his friendly attitude to Belgium and his services as President of the Bank for International Settlements during World War II."(15) This sounds familiar to We The People. Today, bankers on Wall Street who screw up the economy as a whole rarely are held accountable. As it was back then, so it is now.

As World War 2 was ending, in 1945, the United States emerged as a world superpower. This power was not enough to get rid of the BIS. "...in 1945, the BIS outmaneuvered powerful enemies, such as Henry Morganthau, the U.S. Treasury secretary who wanted the bank to be closed down for collaborating with the Nazis."(6) It managed to not only survive the call to be closed, but over the years has gained in power.

In recent times, the BIS has engaged in "helping" banks all around the world. "The BIS, besides being a gathering place for central bank governors, was also the host of an international forum called the Basel Committee on Banking Supervision. More than two dozen countries, including major emerging-market economies, were represented."(16). The BIS has done this three times Basel I was in 1988. Basel II in 2004, and Basel III in 2009. They set the international requirements for bank capital and liquidity.

The theory of this is good – these Basel agreements make banks stronger by forcing them to have larger and better quality reserves so they can weather a downturn better. The dark side however is that by doing this, the banks can lend out less money, and in the short term, this can stagnate an economy. Some have charged that the BIS, with these measures could actually be responsible for recessions in countries where the banks were very weak. By being forced to get stronger, the banks pulled back, and as a result the whole national economy suffered a pullback as a result. It's possible this could be the case, at least to some degree. The second issue is the BIS having the power to force banks around the world to carry out its orders. Nobody elects the BIS directors from the public. The fact that the BIS is not accountable to anyone but has the power to mess in the affairs of sovereign countries around the world is a scary thought. Should the people of the world just trust that the BIS will do the right thing? Their history suggests that they don't always "do the right thing" to put it very charitably. Instead, they choose profit first over We The People of the U.S. and every other nation.

Chapter 11 - Why the government hates gold

We already described how in years past, the U.S. government was a champion of sound money backed by gold and silver. It was the envy of the world. Our currency was also sought all around the world by private citizens and foreign nations. For foreign governments, it made a lot of sense to keep some of their surplus wealth in U.S. dollars. After all, they were backed by gold. So an overseas country could always redeem their currency holdings into the actual gold whenever they wanted. This is one of the main reasons why, even when other countries were coming off the gold standard, the U.S dollar established itself as the Global Reserve Currency – that is, the preferred currency that countries around the world wanted to hold because it had worldwide recognition of value and stability.

The problem is, that while today the U.S. dollar remains the world's preeminent Reserve Currency, the system changed back in 1971. That was the year President Richard Nixon took the U.S. dollar off the gold standard (the dollar had in reality been off the gold standard for U.S. citizens since 1933). Up until 1971, foreign governments could still demand gold in exchange for their dollar reserve holdings if they chose to.

Before 1971, it actually made perfect sense to use the U.S. dollar as the global Reserve Currency. Other nations gobbled up stacks of U.S. dollars. While the dollar continues its role of being the global reserve currency today, the reason for it to be so was removed back in 1971. Today, countries that the U.S. has a large trade imbalance with, namely China, can't be too happy with this system. We as a nation get boatloads of goods manufactured in China where labor is cheap and environmental rules are practically non-existent to fill our superstores like Wal-Mart with. China gets boatloads of our paper money sent to them. Newly printed $100 bills to be exact. That is why, surprisingly, the $100 bill is the second most common denomination of currency right behind the $1 bill. Even though the $100 bill is not seen all that often in commerce within the U.S., it is the favored denomination the government sends overseas to countries like China by the boxload.

The awful truth is the dollar isn't what it used to be. Legendary investor Warren Buffett understands this. In his 2011 Letter to shareholders he remarks that "Even in the U.S., where the wish for a stable currency is strong, the dollar has fallen a staggering 86% in value since 1965...It takes no less than $7 today to buy what $1 did at that time." (1) As a billionaire, it's safe to say that he knows what he's talking about when it comes to money and finance.

Mr. Buffett makes mention of "investments that are denominated in a given currency include money-market funds, bonds, mortgages, bank deposits, and other instruments. Most of these currency-based investments are thought of as "safe." In truth they are among the most dangerous of assets. Their beta maybe zero, but their risk is huge." Mr. Buffett understands that inflation will eat away at the value of money. The truly awful part is that these paper assets are the very assets that the middle class and working class accumulate the most.

Mr. Buffett further elaborates by stating "Over the past century these instruments have destroyed the purchasing power of investors in many countries, even as the holders continued to receive timely payments of interest and principal. This ugly result, moreover, will forever recur. Governments determine the ultimate value of money, and systemic forces will sometimes cause them to gravitate to policies that produce inflation. From time to time such policies spin out of control."

Mr. Buffett knows that not only is the dollar sliding in value over the years, but all the paper investments denominated in these U.S. dollars slide right along with it. You know who else knows this? The Chinese government. A CNN article from Sept 2015 noted that "China owned $1.3 trillion of U.S. Treasuries as of June, making it the biggest holder of U.S. debt."(2)

It just begs the question – how much longer will the Chinese (and other nations for that matter) keep piling on more U.S. government debt and currency that is no longer redeemable in gold and thus is all but guaranteed to lose purchasing power? The U.S. basically imports finished goods from China, and in turn, exports our inflation to them.

The Chinese are pretty smart. They know a thing or two about currency manipulation. This is accomplished by selling their own currency on the foreign exchange market (against dollars) to keep their currency artificially weak on an exchange basis. This makes their exports cheaper and their imports more expensive. Well who cares – why does it matter? Well, by carrying out this manipulation, they hurt the U.S in 2 ways. First, it makes products made in China even cheaper to the outside world (as if the stuff made there isn't cheap enough with using child labor and paying near slave wages). On the surface, this would seem like a good thing – don't we all love cheap crap to buy? Yes, we do...and that's precisely the problem. This is part of why it's not economical for stuff to be manufactured in the U.S. anymore. All those good paying factory jobs have been killed off, and it's still happening today because of this. The policies are stealing American jobs. The second way that it hurts is the flip side: when China imports stuff made in the U.S., those imports are much more expensive than they would otherwise be. So American companies that do make stuff that the people in China want must compete unfairly against Chinese companies which have a big cost advantage. Some of China's 1 billion plus people surely forego buying American made goods because of this, and this goes back again to destroying American manufacturing. With less demand for their products, U.S. companies have less jobs here for American workers. It's actually very simple to understand. The tough part is figuring out what can be done about it. Our politicians haven't been able to come up with a strategy that works to fix this. It probably doesn't help that the Chinese own so much of our country's debt. The Bible says "The rich rule over the poor, and the borrower is slave to the lender"(3). The Chinese are the rich. The U.S. is the borrower and thus the poor slave.

The sad fact is that China could royally screw us all if they wanted to by dumping our debt and currency on the open market en mass. This would hurt them, as the U.S. is their largest customer. It would also hurt them because the value of their own holdings of American currency and debt would plunge as they sold. So I don't think they would go through with this, but one never knows. Iran used the "oil sword" against the U.S. to punish us all in the 1970's. Who really saw that coming back then? I would guess nobody. This would almost certainly mean that interest rates would skyrocket for all of us. Hopefully, this never happens. But the sad fact is our country may not have as much leverage over China as our politicians may have us all believe.

If gold did one thing well, it kept some checks and balances on what the government could do with the money supply. Under the gold standard, the government simply couldn't just decide on a whim to print lots more money to serve their purposes. Also, when the dollar represented gold, it made borrowing much more difficult. Basically the government was restrained by gold. This was a good thing. The government used panics and wars to justify breaking all the rules. The system was too rigid and not flexible enough they proclaimed. Well yes – that was the whole point!

The politicians running the show now probably wish that gold and the gold standard never existed in the first place. That way when they run ramshod over the economy, they wouldn't have any of these pesky doubters pointing to a sound financial system we used to have as a country. They fail to realize that we would never have made it this far to being such a world power if we didn't have such a solid monetary system to start with.

I remember in the 1980's politicians seemed to perennially say how we needed to pay down the national debt. I don't even hear this anymore. You know it's bad when the politicians don't even pay lip service to an issue anymore. They don't even bother pretending. Now, all I hear about is how the U.S. Congress is preparing for yet another fight to raise the debt ceiling so that the country can borrow even more money. As of this writing, the U.S. national debt is $18.9 trillion dollars – that equates to $58,642 for every person in the U.S. – every man, woman and child. If we divide by just the number of *taxpayers* in out nation it gets even more scary – it's $158,276 per taxpayer (4). This doesn't even include all the entitlement debt that exists as obligations stemming from Social Security and Medicare. And the icing on top of this debt cake is that the debt is continuing to go *up*, not down.

Another attribute gold has going for it is the privacy factor. Gold has a high value density to its physical size. You could have tens of thousands of dollars worth in your pocket. What you have is your business. If you own the physical gold, you can do as you wish anonymously. Think about what has happened to paper money now. Most times, it isn't even paper anymore. It's all electronic bits and bytes which can be tracked by the government's snooping eyes. It all creates a paper trail (er, an electronic trail) that can be followed by someone).

But gold is not relevant anymore, government asserts. It is a "Barbarous Relic" from a bygone day. The nation's currency is not backed by gold, nor are the trillions of dollars worth of bonds issued. An interesting fact is that the U.S. Treasury owns 8,140 tons of gold – a figure that hasn't changed in years (5). The Federal Reserve Chairman Ben Bernanke claims it is nothing more than tradition that gold is held(6). Is this believable? Lets look at who owns the most gold around the world:

Note: for a given country, not all its reserves are held as gold. It is usually a mix of gold and the currency of other nations. Below is the amount of gold held by a country or entity and what percentage of their total reserves gold is representing:

WORLD OFFICIAL GOLD HOLDINGS International Financial Statistics, February 2015*(7)

Tonnes ,	% of reserves**
1 United States 8,133.5	72.6%
2 Germany 3,384.2	67.8%
3 IMF 2,814.0	*
4 Italy 2,451.8	66.6%
5 France 2,435.4	65.6%
6 Russia 1,208.2	12.2%
7 China 1,054.1	1.0%
8 Switzerland 1,040.0	7.7%
9 Japan 765.2	2.4%
10 Netherlands 612.5	55.2%
11 India 557.7	6.7%
12 Turkey6) 529.1	16.1%
13 ECB 503.2	26.5% (European Central Bank)
14 Taiwan 423.6	3.9%
15 Portugal 382.5	75.3%
16 Venezuela 367.6	69.3%
17 Saudi Arabia 322.9	1.7%
18 United Kingdom 310.3	11.2%
19 Lebanon 286.8	21.5%
20 Spain 281.6	21.7%
21 Austria 280.0	43.4%

22 Belgium 227.4	34.7%
23 Philippines 195.1	9.6%
24 Kazakhstan 191.8	25.7%
25 Algeria 173.6	3.5%
26 Thailand 152.4	3.8%
27 Singapore 127.4	1.9%
28 Sweden 125.7	7.8%
29 South Africa 125.2	9.9%
30 Mexico 122.7	2.4%

* IMF balance sheets do not allow this percentage to be calculated

Looking at just the top 30 largest holders of gold, it appears that gold has a worldwide appeal to nations around the world. Top holders are located in the Americas, Europe, Asia, and Africa. The countries include both wealthy first world nations as well as poor third world nations. They all hold gold reserves.

Interestingly, there is no currency in the world backed by gold. The last country to back their currency with gold was Switzerland in 1999 when their money had a partial backing with gold. This could be one of the greatest conspiracies in the world. They all basically hate gold when it comes to having citizens hold gold and trade gold. But judging from their actions of holding so much gold, they all share one trait: the governments of the world all love gold themselves – so long as it's in *their* vaults.

Chapter 12 - Why the banks hate gold – the big and *not* so mighty banks

When we think of companies, we have a general idea of what they do to make the money they earn. They borrow money to construct a factory. They hire workers to run these plants, and they start making a product. The product is then distributed to the masses. If people like the product, the company will do well, and take their excess profits to reward the owners of the company. They may reinvest in the business to generate even more money in the future. Service companies do the same thing, except substitute product for a certain service they provide.

What happens if the role of money is not just the result of your product or service? What happens if your product is money itself? This is what banks do – they take in money as deposits and lend money as loans, hoping to make money on their money.

The problem with banks is they don't own their product the way other companies do. Manufacturing companies really own their product – they design it, make it, distribute it. They can outsource one or more of these functions, but the bottom line is they own the products that they sell. For banks, nothing can be further from the truth. The banks have money to lend because they have deposits from people. Those deposits from people – all the checking, savings accounts, certificate of deposits, - all of them are liabilities to the bank. They are an asset to the depositor, but to the bank they are a debt. It is this money they use to lend to other people. So they do not really own even the money they are lending out. They borrow most of their product. On top of the debt from the deposits, the big banks issue many bonds to borrow on the corporate level. Banks use fractional-reserve banking, meaning they loan out the money they take in, and hold only a fraction of what the deposits are in cash. The more loaned out, the more money a bank makes.

On some basic level, the banks have a very simple formula for making profits. They borrow for x percent interest and loan the same money at y percent interest and keep the difference (the spread) for themselves as their profit. So if a bank takes in $100,000 and pays the depositor 3% interest and then takes this money and lends it out at 7% interest, then the bank makes the 4% spread on the $100,000 or $4,000 profit. Not too shabby! It seems like a perfect business – it seems so simple!

But it's not simple. Investors found out the hard way in the Great Recession of 2009 that banks can be inherently weak. The scary part is that investors don't know how strong or weak a bank is until it is tested by a bad economy. A reason for this is the debts on a bank's balance sheet are relatively fixed – deposits, plus corporate debts, plus any other obligations created from trading equals an enormous sum of money that the bank owes. And the bigger the bank, the more money they owe, so size here is not always an advantage. Meanwhile on the asset side of the balance sheet, the banks have the loans that they made – what other people owe them. These loans outstanding are the principle asset of the bank. The trouble is trying to value a collection of these loans made by the bank and figure out what they are actually worth.

It stands to reason that when times are good, the banks make some handsome profits on their assets. The stocks in big banks will be high giving big banks giant market values, usually with a generous dividend payout. As soon as bad times come, loans start to be delinquent or default. The loans the bank made (their Assets) will start to be viewed suspiciously by investors. People start wondering if maybe the bank didn't make wise loans in their quest to get bigger and bigger profits. The assets on the balance sheet start looking shaky. If enough of these loans go into default, then the bank goes bankrupt.

This can all happen extremely fast. The economy can, and does, go from good to bad like that – a few hiccups here and there and next thing you know, the sky is falling. What started as a problem in the niche market of subprime mortgages at the end of 2007, quickly spread to prime mortgages, consumer credit and commercial credit in 2008 and 2009. Some of the biggest banks in the country were kept alive by taking money from the U.S. government because they were deemed 'to big to fail" for the good of the economy.

In this troubled time, the value of the assets the banks rested on were simply overvalued – the true value was nowhere near the kind of money the banks had originally lent out. This caused the banks to write down the value of their loans on their balance sheet. But the debt the bank *owes* doesn't get written down. The banks were all talking about how homeowners were underwater – they owed more than their homes were now worth. The truth is that a lot of the banks were now underwater. The thin amount of equity they had in their own operations was now wiped out. Because of fractional reserve banking, the banks had loaned out far too much, and held reserves that were far too little, causing a liquidity crisis. This is why the government stepped in to bail them out.

Because of the nature of a bank's business, a bank can never really be as strong as a manufacturer can be. This isn't to say that all manufacturing companies are financially sound. Far from it. But manufacturers *can* be financially stronger than the biggest of banks. The value of a bank's assets are always in flux. It depends on interest rates, investor sentiment, loan default rates, and many other metrics used to analyze banks.

Lets look at an example of a bank versus a manufacturer. We'll look at Bank of America, one of the largest U.S. banks versus Tootsie Roll Industries, a U.S. based candy manufacturer(1) (Author's disclosure: I own shares in Tootsie Roll Industries):

Bank of America results for 2006 (before the economic crisis):

Net Profit: $21.13 Billion

Share price: between $40.90 to $55.1 per share

Approximate Market cap based on share price: $182 Billion to $245 Billion

Dividends declared per share: $2.12 per share

Average price to earnings ratio: 10.8

Average shares outstanding: 4.45 billion shares

From this data in 2006, it seems that Bank of America would be solid. The stock market is valuing the bank at a couple hundred billion dollars depending on the share price at any particular moment. It also seems like it's not very expensive – paying 10.8 times a firm's earnings isn't a very high price to become an owner or increase our ownership stake in it. Let's see how it fared for 2009 during the Great Recession

Bank of America results for 2009 (during the economic crisis):

Net Profit $6.27 Billion

Share price: between per share $2.5 to $19.1 per share

Approximate Market cap based on share price: $ 21 billion to $165 billion

Dividends declared per share: 4 cents per share

Average price to earnings ratio: Not meaningful

Average shares outstanding: 8.65 billion shares

Comparing these figures, we can see that an investment in Bank of America did not go so smoothly. The investors lost billions of dollars worth of share value, and the bank reduced their dividend payout to almost nothing. To top it off, the number of shares increased to such a degree that it resulted in an almost doubling the number outstanding. This is not good – your ownership stake in the bank would have fallen by almost 100% as they issued more shares. This is called dilution and is not a good thing – you will have a smaller share of the profits going into the future (the pie has to be split among many more shares). As bad as the numbers look for 2009, the very next year in 2010, Bank of America made no income at all – they actually had a net LOSS of $2.23 Billion.

Lets compare this against a stodgy old candy manufacturer

Tootsie Roll Industries results for 2006 (before the economic crisis)(2):

Net Profit: $65.9 million

Share price: between $20.1 to $26 per share

Approximate Market cap based on share price: $ 1.4 billion to 1.82 billion

Dividends declared per share: 24 cents per share

Average price to earnings ratio: 24.1

Average shares outstanding: shares 70.13 million

It seems that in 2006 Tootsie Roll Industries is a small to midsize firm doing what it has done for several decades – producing candy under the brand names such as Tootsie Rolls, Tootsie Pops, Sugar Daddy, Charms, Charleston Chew, Junior Mints, Andes Candies (my personal favorite) among others. How would they survive in the brutal recession that was right around the corner? Let's see:

Tootsie Roll Industries results for 2009 (during the economic crisis):

Net Profit: $53.5 million

Share price: between $15.9 to $23.5 per share

Approximate Market cap based on share price: $ 1.0 billion to $1.5 billion

Dividends declared per share: 26 cents per share

Average price to earnings ratio: 24.9

Average shares outstanding: shares 66.53 million

This shows us that while earnings did decline somewhat, the share price wasn't decimated to the same degree that befell Bank of America's shares. Also notice a few other distinctions. First, management had enough confidence in the strength of the company to not only maintain the dividend to investors, but rather to *increase* payouts in the face of one of the worst recessions in decades. Second, notice that the *number of shares declined* – the company was busy buying back its own shares for the benefit of the existing stockholders that stayed the course and didn't sell. So in the end, the shareholders own that much more of the company. Third, investors must have been somewhat happy with all this, because the average price to earnings multiple edged up slightly – indicating that investors did not punish the company for its performance, but rather were more willing to pay even more money to obtain a piece of the company.

Lets look at the capital structure of both companies. For Tootsie Roll Industries on 6/30/2015, it had a total debt of only $8.2 million (and of this, $7.5 million of which was capitalized leases), so it has almost no debt. Based on their lowered earnings of $53 million, they could pay off their entire debt burden in 2 months time if they chose to. How about Bank of America? On 6/30/2015 it had Long term debt of $243.4 Billion! Even if they make $21 billion a year like in the good old days (they haven't been able to yet) it would take over a decade to pay off this giant debt load –and that's only if they used every penny of earnings to do nothing but pay off debt.

This comparison between these two firms should illustrate one thing: that banks are extremely dependent on debt. Bank of America in all likelihood will never pay off that debt – they probably would not even try. Again, they are in the business of borrowing money and then lending out that borrowed money. Think about that the next time you think of one of these giant banks being so large and mighty. It is not just Bank of America either. Lets see how much long term debt other large banks have on their balance sheets (3):

Citigroup - $211.8 Billion on 6/30/2015

JPMorgan Chase & Co: $286.7 Billion on 6/30/2015

Wells Fargo & Co: $179.8 Billion on 6/30/2015

The Key to all of this: The banking sector needs massive amounts of debt in order to make profits. This is at the heart of why banks hate deflation and love inflation. The banks will have to pay back all of this debt they are saddled with. In a deflationary economy, the currency is gaining strength and increasing in purchasing power. The banks don't like this. They don't like the scenario of having to pay out a dollar in the future that will be worth more than it is today. The banks will always support an inflationary monetary policy. In a way, this is the only rational thing for them to do – to make projections of paying their debts with currency that is consistently losing its value.

Gold has been the ultimate guarantor of stable money. As such, it represents a threat to the dollar as a competitor. What threatens the dollar threatens the product of the bank, and thus the bank itself. It has long been rumored that the banks act in concert with governments to try to suppress the price of gold for this reason. It has been documented that banks do trade gold on the COMEX (the gold futures market). It's interesting to note that when trading futures, it's paper they are trading, not actually the physical gold changing hands. Selling futures contracts on the open market would have a suppressing effect on the gold price, even without physical exchange occurring. It would be in the bank's interest (especially the central banks) to do exactly this.

Chapter 13 - Big Banks Behaving Badly

There is a theme in this book that banks behave badly. It runs through the whole book in many of the chapters. Why is that? For starters, the bigger the bank, the worse they seem to behave. They just give us all so many examples of their bad actions that a writer could write a whole book on just this one topic. In fact, I don't think one book would be enough to contain even half the shenanigans they pull. It would take a set of books resembling the old encyclopedias we all used to use before the internet. This was one of the easiest chapters to do research on because there is just so much material that exists. The hardest part was narrowing it down to just a few examples that would give us a chapter and not a book.

Keep in mind, in almost all cases, when we're talking about the banks, we are speaking of the biggest banks. Nobody is beating up on the local community bank where the bank manager and tellers know your name and give your kids lollipops while telling you they'll see you at the annual town day picnic. This is the image of banking at its best. Where they are genuinely part of the community they serve.

What we are focusing on are the biggest banks of all. These big banks are goliaths. They are usually located on or near Wall Street, not Main Street. They always have this tendency to do the wrong thing. With all their financial resources at their disposal, one would like to think that these giant banks would take the high road.

That they would behave ethically in the name of good, solid business, as this would ensure them of long term profits by treating customers fairly and squarely.

What has happened is the opposite. The biggest and most powerful of the banks have set their eyes on quick profits without regards to long term consequences. It seems like they have a real knack at sizing up situations and doing exactly what is wrong for their customers, wrong for the communities, wrong for the economy, and wrong for the nation. This is all the more terrifying when you consider that these large banks literally own the Federal Reserve, and thus have a hand in deciding vital aspects of our economy. Aspects such as the supply of money and interest rates are controlled by the Fed, which in turn is owned and controlled by these big banks. One would think that these big banks would at the least be patriotic and put our nation first. Sadly, this is rarely, if ever, true. They put short term profits for themselves first and foremost.

All of this has not been lost on We The People. These big banks are not pulling the wool over our eyes. Most Americans hate the big banks because they all recognize that We The People get screwed by them. Even the National Review which is generally considered a conservative, pro-business publication recognizes this fact: "Everybody hates bankers, and they're a hateable bunch: After making a series of insanely hubristic bets on the U.S. housing market, they created a credit crisis and helped set off an ugly recession...The big banks took billions in bailout loans at sweetheart rates and used a fair bit of the subsequent profits to finance the presidential campaign of Barack Obama, with Goldman Sachs becoming the Democrats' largest business donor in 2008."(1)

Public Opinion of the big banks has gotten so bad that nobody can really defend them. Even pro-business publications have come clean and admitted that we all harbor some degree of hatred toward them. It's no surprise that Goldman Sachs is named right off the bat. You have to ask yourself...*why* was Goldman Sachs the largest business donor for the Democrats during 2008? This was the election year that President Obama was seeking re-election. But just think of all the businesses out there that make huge profits – was Goldman Sachs making that much more money than all the other businesses that they could just throw money around? Lets examine how much money Goldman Sachs made in profit and compare this against what other big businesses earned in 2008: (2)

Company	Net Profit for 2008
Goldman Sachs	$2.3 Billion
Morgan Stanley	$1.8 Billion
American Express	$2.8 Billion
Visa	$1.7 Billion
JPMorgan Chase	$3.6 Billion
Bank of America	$4.0 Billion
Altria	$3.4 Billion
Philip Morris Int'l	$6.8 Billion
Wal-Mart	$13.5 Billion
3M Company	$3.4 Billion

Proctor & Gamble	$12.0 Billion
Coca-Cola	$7.0 Billion
PepsiCo	$5.1 Billion
Johnson & Johnson	$12.9 Billion
McDonald's	$4.2 Billion
BP	$25.5 Billion
Chevron	$23.9 Billion
Exxon Mobil	$45.2 Billion

We can see that Goldman Sachs was quite profitable in 2008. It was not the most profitable company, not by a long shot. But it was the biggest donor to the Democrats, who had a sitting president running for re-election. I compared the profits of Goldman Sachs against other large companies. Notice that some of these other companies operate in industries that people in general dislike. Three of the companies – Exxon Mobil, Chevron, and BP are all oil companies. People don't really love oil companies, especially when gas prices are high. (In particular, BP has a tarnished reputation resulting from their Deepwater Horizon oil spill, but this happened later, in 2010). All three oil companies made over 10 times the amount of profit in 2008 compared to Goldman. Yet it was Goldman contributing more money. Altria and Philip Morris Int'l are tobacco giants. Big Tobacco has a public relations issue – the tobacco industry doesn't have lots of fans among the public. Both these firms made more profit than Goldman in 2008. Yet again, Goldman Sachs gave more money to the Democratic Party.

Why was Goldman Sachs so generous in re-electing President Obama? While very profitable, we have proven that it is not because it was the most profitable company. Other companies that made far more money and had reputations just as bad were not giving at the same level, so what gives? It is obvious – Goldman Sachs was paying what amounts to a bribe...what else do you call it when you pay money to politicians who have a hand regulating you? You pay and they leave you alone so you can continue making your ill-begotten profits.

Goldman Sachs has powerful friends in addition to the presidency. They are the ultimate establishment when it comes to the Federal Reserve..."Geithner's close ties to the Wall Street elite was evidenced in a report in the Wall Street Journal on May 4, 2009, describing how the chair of the New York Federal Reserve Bank, Stephen Friedman, had made millions off his purchase of Goldman Sachs stock, a violation of Federal Reserve policy after Goldman – to qualify for government bailout funds-became a bank holding company. Geithner was then the New York Fed president, and he was complicit in approving that deal. When Friedman bought stock in Goldman, the company he once headed and where he still was a director, he was hoping for a waiver of the stock ownership ban to permit him to hold his existing multimillion-dollar stock stash and to remain on the Goldman board. Geithner requested the waiver the previous October. Yet, without having received that waiver, Friedman went ahead in December and purchased 37,300 additional Goldman shares. With shares he added in January, a day after the waiver was granted, he ended up with 98,600 shares in Goldman Sachs, worth a total of $13,330,720 at the time of the Wall Street Journal Report...Friedman was in violation of the Fed's policy because, thanks in part to the urging of

Geithner and the New York Fed, Goldman Sachs was allowed to become a bank holding company, making it eligible for government bailout funds (an option that Geithner had denied to Goldman rival Lehman Brothers). But that shift also put Goldman under more rigorous banking regulations that required Friedman, as a Class C director of the New York Fed, a position in which he ostensibly represents the public instead of the banks that dominate the board, to step down as a Goldman director and divest his holdings. Instead, he stayed on the Goldman board and added additional shares while waiting for the Fed waiver. Nor did he inform the Federal Reserve of his additional purchases in December, and the lawyers for the New York Fed didn't know about that purchase until the Journal raised questions the following April. Friedman made a profit of about $3 million on the additional shares...Goldman received speedy approval to become a bank holding company in September and a $10 billion capital injection soon after."(3)

Well, of course Goldman got what it wanted. When it didn't qualify to receive the bailout money, it got to change all the rules to get it. They got to not only change their corporate structure to get the approval, but a *speedy* approval at that. And why not? The people running the Fed were too busy illegally speculating in Goldman Sachs stock to enrich themselves. It's bad enough that these men didn't do their jobs, but the fact that they were playing with Goldman stock for their own personal benefit is just crazy. Remember that Mr. Friedman was the man who supposedly represented the interests of the public on the Fed's board. He owned millions of dollars worth of Goldman Sachs stock. How could he possibly be impartial? He can't be. If you or I did this stuff, we would be going to jail. For the men who run the show, it's just another day of business as usual.

Goldman Sachs, as mentioned elsewhere in this book, has embraced Hillary Clinton by paying her over $200,000 per speech for 3 speeches she made to them. If it wasn't for Senator Bernie Sanders bringing up this issue, we would most likely not have found out that she raked in more than $600,000 for a few speeches. As of this writing, she has resisted attempts by Senator Sanders calling on her to release the transcripts of those speeches. Goldman knows a good thing when they've got it. They effectively have already started greasing the wheels of Hillary Clinton to no doubt continue the cozy relationship they have with the presidency of President Obama. They want to continue having their gravy train rolling at full speed after Obama leaves office. As mentioned elsewhere, Goldman settled and paid up to a roughly $5 billion fine in January 2016 for its role in the faulty mortgage mess from seven years ago. None of their executives will face any jail time or even any prosecution.

The big banks getting preferential treatment isn't limited to Goldman. Citigroup received a special temporary waiver from Glass-Steagall. "Enacted as part of the Banking Act in 1933 in response to the Great Depression, Glass-Steagall imposed a separation between investment banking and commercial banking. This prevented federally backed deposits in commercial banks -- the type the public uses -- from being used to finance the much riskier activities of investment banks. The problem is that with the government guaranteeing deposits in commercial banks, investors have no incentive to monitor the ways those banks use their deposits. That gives banks the freedom to undertake highly risky ventures without having to worry that depositors will move their money elsewhere. If the ventures are successful, the payoff is large. If they fail, the government covers the losses. Heads the bank wins, tails the taxpayer loses."(4) In the case of Citigroup, "The regulators at the Fed and elsewhere went along with the grand proposal, giving the new company a two-year waiver from compliance with Glass-Steagall. Thanks in part to Citigroup's lobbying and the enthusiasm of the media, Congress would replace Glass-Steagall entirely a year later."(5)

It's not just big American banks that can behave badly either. Probably the most notorious bank ever was the Bank of Credit & Commerce International (BCCI). Even though it has a generic sounding name, read an excerpt about the bank: "Nothing in the history of modern financial scandals rivals the unfolding saga of the *Bank of Credit & Commerce International (B.C.C.I.)* the $20 billion rogue empire that regulators in 62 countries shut down early this month *(July 1991)* in a stunning global sweep. Never has a single scandal involved so much money, so many nations or so many prominent people... it is the largest corporate criminal enterprise ever, the biggest Ponzi scheme, the most pervasive money-laundering operation and financial supermarket ever created for the likes of Manuel Noriega, Ferdinand Marcos, Saddam Hussein and the Colombian drug barons... a clandestine division of the bank called the "black network," which functions as a global intelligence operation and a Mafia-like enforcement squad. Operating primarily out of the bank's offices in Karachi, Pakistan, the 1,500-employee black network has used sophisticated spy equipment and techniques, along with bribery, extortion, kidnapping and even, by some accounts, murder. The black network - so named by its own members - stops at almost nothing to further the bank's aims the world over. The more conventional departments of B.C.C.I. handled such services as laundering money for the drug trade and helping dictators loot their national treasuries. The black network, which is still functioning,(authors note: this article is from 1991, and the BCCI no longer exists) operates a lucrative arms-trade business and transports drugs and gold. According to investigators and participants in those operations, it often works with Western and Middle Eastern intelligence agencies. The strange and still murky ties between B.C.C.I. and the intelligence agencies of several countries are so pervasive that even the White House has become entangled."(6). Interestingly, gold was a relevant commodity to even this bank which was clearly involved in all kinds of criminal activities.

I bring this up also to show just how bad things can get in the absence or non-enforcement of laws. Just imagine: your credit card company coming after you with assassins instead of lawyers. Big Bank Behavior can always get worse. This bank was so criminal and did things that were so crazy that it drew the attention of Hollywood. The 2009 film called "The International" is based on this bank. In the movie, the name was changed to the International Bank of Business and Credit (IBBC) and portrays how the bank funds arms trading, money laundering, terrorism, and rebel groups. (Author's note: if you like action films, it's pretty good).

The BCCI wasn't some small fringe bank. They were really an international bank. They even operated here in the U.S. "Front men often stood in to mask the identity of the real borrowers or purchasers. The Federal Reserve Board believes that the use of front men ultimately enabled B.C.C.I. to buy control of First American Bankshares Inc.,...Bankers, regulators and even some law-enforcement officials had only vague notions for years that the BCC Group S.A., the holding company for B.C.C.I. and its affiliates, was a strange and shadowy institution. Since the early 1980's, the company's reputation made banking officials uneasy -- a "stateless" bank that operated in the United States and about 70 other countries, chartered in Luxembourg, run by Pakistanis, owned by Arabs, headquartered in Britain and serviced by outposts in the Cayman Islands, a well-known haven for private banking. Police and intelligence experts nicknamed B.C.C.I. the "Bank of Crooks and Criminals" for its penchant for catering to customers who dealt in arms, drugs and hot money... The most visible B.C.C.I. front man in the United States, according to the Federal Reserve Board, was Ghaith R. Pharaon, a Harvard-trained Saudi businessman who has owned banks, hotels and manufacturing businesses around the world, including extensive projects in Argentina. From his estate in Richmond Hill, GA., near Savannah, Mr. Pharaon befriended wealthy American politicans and business leaders, including former Atlanta Mayor Andrew Young and Bert Lance, the Georgia banker who served as budget director in the Carter Administration... The bank curried favor with other prominent people through charitable donations or consulting fees, including former President Jimmy Carter and former Prime Minster James Callaghan of Britain, to lend B.C.C.I. an aura of influence and respectability."(7)

If there is one take away from this whole chapter, then I think the last sentence you read sums it up. For big and powerful banks it's all about buying themselves access to elected leaders. This is what gives them control, influence, and at least on the surface, respectability. This is true for all banks whether they are dealing in guns, assassins, and drugs or they are dealing in stocks, bonds, and derivatives from Wall Street.

Chapter 14 - What happens when paper money fails? Weimer Germany

I imagine some people are thinking along on these lines: "yeah, if the paper money starts to all in out fail it would be bad – we would all lose purchasing power and that would not be good for anyone. At least nobody would actually get hurt though. Not in the real, physical sense. It would just be a bad economy. We (the government, or people or companies or someone) would just change the money we use and life will go on. Everything would be OK. " But, would that be what actually happens?

We have a case in which paper money failed that we can study to see how things turned out. Better than that, it's not ancient history in some far corner of the earth from 5,000 years ago. We have a relatively modern economy to look at.

Back in the late 19th century and early 20th century, Germany was a giant. It was a powerhouse in science and medicine. Its economy was industrialized. The people had a strong work ethic. This was no backwater. The country was a first world nation back then (as it is today). Then Germany started the Great War (later known as World War I). Unfortunately for Germany and their citizens, they lost. This is where all the troubles for them started.

After the war, the allies, led by Great Britain and France demanded "War Reparations" – money to be paid by Germany to compensate them for the war. They asserted that Germany started the war, was at fault for all this damage and death, and now that they had beaten

Germany, Germany was going to have to pay –literally. Oh, and one more thing – the Allies really knew what they were doing in those days. They wouldn't take any funny money paper currency either. They wanted to be paid in gold. "In April 1921 the Allies had presented Germany the bill for reparations, a whopping 132 billion gold marks – 33 billion dollars – which the Germans howled they could not possibly pay. The mark (the German currency), normally valued at four to the dollar, had begun to fall; by the summer of 1921 it had dropped to seventy-five, a year later to four hundred, to the dollar..."(1)

As perceptions are the only thing holding up a paper currency's value, it's no wonder the money started to fall right away. Everyone, both inside and outside Germany knew they were in real trouble. Faith started to melt faster than an ice cream cone on a hot July day. "...certain deliveries in kind – coal, ships, lumber, cattle, etc, - were to be made in lieu of cash reparations."(2). It was spelled out – Germany was either going to pay the gold or if they couldn't, start giving up their "stuff" of value. The Allies weren't letting them off the hook, no matter what.

Germany, during this messy period after World War I, was ruled by a weak democratic government called the Weimer Republic. "The fledgling Weimer Republic was in deep trouble, its very existence constantly threatened not only from the extreme Right but from the extreme Left"(1).

This makes sense – when everything is going to hell in a handbag, people have a way of becoming very mad and angry. When people get like this, they start paying attention to the fringe elements of the political spectrum. They want change – drastic change NOW! The feeling is that the government is doing so bad, how can these radical people running for office do any worse – give them a shot.

"The masses of the people, however, did not realize how much the industrial tycoons, the Army and the State were benefiting from the ruin of the currency. All they knew was that a large bank account could not buy a straggly bunch of carrots, a half peck of potatoes, a few ounces sugar, a pound of flour. They knew that as individuals they were bankrupt. And they knew hunger when it gnawed at them, as it did daily. In their misery and hopelessness they made the Republic the scapegoat for all that had happened. Such times were heaven-sent for Adolf Hitler".(3),

One would think that the wealthy would have the most to lose. As crazy as it sounds, the big money players actually came out ahead. The big companies and the German government were heavily in debt and by making the currency worth less and less, they easily and cheaply got rid of their debts. "...though the masses of the people were financially ruined, the government deliberately let the mark tumble in order to free the State of its public debts...moreover, the destruction of the currency enabled German heavy industry to wipe out its indebtedness by refunding its obligations in worthless marks."(3). Even in this crazy situation, big government and big companies were in bed together because they shared a mutual interest in erasing their debts.

"...in the fall of 1922 the German government had asked the Allies to grant a moratorium on reparation payments. This the French government of Poincare had bluntly refused. When Germany defaulted in deliveries of timber, the hardheaded French Premier, who had been the wartime president of France, ordered French troops to occupy the Ruhr. The Industrial heart of Germany, which after the loss of Upper Silesia to Poland, furnished the Reich with four fifths of its coal and steel production, was cut off from the rest of the country...The strangulation of Germany's economy hastened the final plunge of the mark. On the occupation of the Ruhr in January 1923, it fell to 18,000 to the dollar; by July 1 it had dropped to 160,000; by August 1 to a million. By November, when Hitler thought his hour had struck, it took four billion marks to buy a dollar, and thereafter the figures became trillions. German currency had become utterly worthless. Purchasing power of salaries and wages was reduced to zero. The life savings of the middle classes and the working classes were wiped out. But something even more important was destroyed: the faith of the people in the economic structure of German society. What good were the standards and practices of such a society, which encouraged savings and investment and solemnly promised a safe return from them and then defaulted? Was this not a fraud upon the people?"(6) Yes it was. The German people learned the hard way that all paper money is inherently a fraud.

Things had gone from bad to worse. Then got only worse again. The paper money was in a state of utter collapse. "By the fall of 1923 , Hitler was openly calling for a revolt against the government. Inflation had turned into hyperinflation...on November 8, the night of what would go down in history as the beginning of the Beer Hall Putsch, the price of the three beers he ordered was three *billion* marks"(4)

Think about how bad the money situation had gotten – just a couple of years ago a mark was worth some 25 Cents American (that's a quarter made of *real silver* by the way). Now in 1923 it took a billion marks to buy a single beer! Even Hitler, who saw this as his opportunity to try to seize power for himself must have been beside himself with this level of currency collapse. When "The government calmly goes on printing these scraps of paper because, if it stopped, that would be the end of the government" he (Adolph Hitler) cried out"(3).

Hitler hit the nail on the head with his comment. We can see that Hitler's choice of words to describe the currency – as "scraps of paper" fitted the mood of the people. They were not even worthy of being called notes or anything else. The farce that inherently is paper money was in full view.

The often told story of the wheelbarrow full of money comes from this period. The story goes that someone is pushing stacks of paper money in a wheelbarrow on the way to the store. They take a break of some kind, and when they return, they find the currency dumped out on the ground, and the wheelbarrow has been stolen. The moral here is the wheelbarrow has some value and is worth stealing. The money is essentially worth nothing – it's not even worth the labor of lugging the paper.

In the end, we know how this whole chaotic mess got "solved". Germany elected Adolph Hitler in 1933, to become Chancellor. Germany got Hitler and the Nazi party running their country. The Jews got persecuted and then ultimately got genocide. The whole world got war. Not just any war, but World War 2 which resulted in at least 60 million people dead.(7)

It's not that all this economic upheaval created Hitler per se. Hitler and others like him would most likely have had their radical ideas even if this had been the best of times. But people wouldn't have given him the time of day if everything had been OK. The currency collapse was a driving force for making people angry and searching out radical candidates like Hitler who promised them stability and greatness for their country. They got some of what they wanted in the beginning as Germany started bullying other countries to give it concessions. But ultimately the whole world paid an awful price.

Chapter 15 - Is gold money today?

"Money is gold, and nothing else" – J.P. Morgan(1)

J.P. Morgan probably never envisioned the day when governments went out of their way to decouple "money" from "gold". Likewise our nation's founding fathers who signed off on the United States Constitution are probably rolling over in their graves. They knew what they were doing when they spelled out that gold and silver should be the money of the land.

A year ago, I read a book on gold called "Gold – the Race for the World's most seductive metal" by Matthew Hart. I took exception to only one issue in the book – the conclusion that gold and money are different. On page 171 it says "The idea that gold is universal money is laughable. Who would accept it? It would have to be someone with testing equipment at his elbow. It's not easy to sell gold". On pages 172-173 Mr. Hart backs up his assertion with a story of London criminals that rob a bank vault they think will have currency, but instead find and steal 6,800 bars of gold. "Gold is not money. If they had found the stash of banknotes they'd expected, they would have stuffed it in gym bags, gone home, and divvied it up in the basement. The only skill required was counting. But gold's conversion into money demands a different skill set, which the thieves did not possess. You could say that, right away, they found themselves facing the liquidity challenge of a precious metal. A thing is liquid if there is a ready market for it, as there is for gold. But it's not a market that you and your mates can drop your gold at on the way back from the depot." This book was good, especially at looking at gold mining, except for these three pages and the conclusions the author draws from them. I took the unusual step of actually emailing my thoughts about this to Mr. Hart. He was kind enough to respond, which I will not print here since I did not ask for permission to reprint it. Suffice it to say, the author stuck to his original positions.

The first issue is that he does not consider gold universal money – he thinks it laughable. We all know you can't walk into a Wal-Mart and pay with gold (well, actually you can – if it is an old U.S. gold coin with a monetary value on it, you CAN do exactly this – it's the law in fact. It is still legal tender. You would be crazy to do it as the value of the gold would far exceed the face value of the coin.). So for practical purposes, you "can't" do it. But, you can easily sell the gold and in return receive the paper currency which you could use at any store you choose. It is not only money, but the most universal money there is. You could carry out this exchange for local currency in any country, not just the United States. Gold is one of only a handful of "things" that you can trade for local currency, whether you're in Canada, South Africa, Saudi Arabia, India, France., Mexico, you name it.

Mr. Hart asks "Who would accept it?" "It's not easy to sell gold". I should have asked him whether he has ever actually bought or sold physical gold. Even though he has written a whole book on the subject, his conclusions make me think the answer is no. (to be fair again to him, his short biography does say that he is a writer and journalist. It says nothing of him being a bullion trader or coin collector or anything else that would give him a background in actually handling the metal). I have personally bought/sold so let me answer this question "Who would accept it?" From my experience, everyone wants gold. The only reason someone wouldn't accept it is if they're ignorant of the true value, and therefore afraid of getting ripped off. Anyone with experience would know the approximate worth. In every city of a somewhat decent size, there are people buying and selling gold. Mr. Hart makes the comment "It's not easy to sell gold". He's wrong. He is just flat out wrong on this. Big cities have actual bullion stores where all they do is buy and sell precious metals. Now, you can even sell to reputable companies by mail that handle huge volumes of precious metals of all types. Also, coin shops everywhere will want to buy gold from you. The tiniest little rundown hole in the wall coin shop that you would think has no money to offer....bring them a gold item, especially a gold coin - and see how fast cash comes out to make you an offer. Smaller cities have jewelry stores that will buy your gold items. It is their business. All of these establishments will know what your gold is worth. Most are honest. A handful will try to take advantage of you by buying on the cheap if they think you don't know what you're doing. All these places do have testing equipment on hand – they use them to perform an acid test on chains and rings. If we're talking a gold coin, they won't bother. They will know just by weighing it. Due to the weight density of gold, It's extremely hard to fake a gold coin – once you get used to seeing and feeling the real thing, you know a fake just by seeing and feeling it.

Mr. Hart speaks of the "liquidity challenge of a precious metal". I can tell you that this does not exist at all with gold. Mr. Hart uses a bad example about criminals that just stole gold bars to back him up. All I can say is that if you have any stolen goods, people will be weary of buying from you if they have suspicion. In this case when it's all over the news the next day that thousands of bars have been stolen from some bank, then yeah, if you walk into anywhere with all these gold bars and don't seem to have much knowledge when the buyer is asking you about them, they're not going to buy (well, again some are dishonest dealers and may still try to purchase it real cheap). In these cases, it's not the gold, it's the fact that nobody reputable wants to deal in stolen merchandise. Even if you steal currency, from some banks anyway, the serial numbers on the notes may be consecutive at the large banks, and the police will be able to track your movements as you spend it all over the place.

The fact that a professional journalist can write a book all about gold and come to these conclusions that gold isn't money shows just how effective the disinformation the Fed and the government has spread has been. "The shot that started the modern gold war was U.S. President Richard Nixon's removal of the world's reserve currency, the U.S. dollar, from its international peg with gold on August 15, 1971...By default, on that day gold became the anti-currency to the U.S. dollar and the rest of the world's fiat currencies. Perception management – what we call public relations today – kicked into high gear."(3)

The deception and disinformation isn't limited to books by journalists either. When congressman Ron Paul asked Federal Reserve chairman Ben Bernanke:

" When you wake up in the morning, do you think about the price of gold," Rep. Paul asked. After pausing for a second, Bernanke responded, clearly uncomfortable. that he paid much attention to the price of gold, only to be interrupted once again. "Gold's at about $1,580 [an ounce] this morning, what do you think of the price of gold?" asked Rep. Paul. A stern-faced Bernanke responded people bought it for protection and was once again cut-off, with Ron Paul once again on the offensive.

When congressman Ron Paul asked Federal Reserve chairman Ben Bernanke "Is gold money? "Clearly bothered, Bernanke told the representative, "No. it's a precious metal". After Paul interrupted him to note the long history of gold being used as money, Bernanke continued "it's an asset. Would you say Treasury bills are money? I don't think they're money either but they're a financial asset". Paul asked Bernanke why central banks didn't hold diamonds, clearly hinting at his fiat money criticism of the U.S. monetary system. The Fed chairman told Rep Paul it was nothing more than tradition..."(4)

Could it be that the Fed chairman harbors some logical reasons for keeping gold in central banks? Perhaps Bernanke isn't telling the whole truth in this exchange with Congress. In fact, one may even think that by saying the reason central banks keep gold was "nothing more than tradition" Bernanke may have come dangerously close to perjuring himself to Congress the way he prefaced it as the only reason. Does he *really* believe what he is telling Congress?

If he does believe it, it would imply that gold is just trivial. But if gold is trivial, why would the Fed chairman say that he pays "much attention" to the price of gold? It doesn't add up. Bernanke goes on to say people buy it for protection. Might that be the real reason the U.S. government also holds gold – for protection on a national scale? It seems to me that gold, as the universal money would be a perfect form of money to have just in case of a war or other major disaster our country could face. Our currency could be refused by other nations but they may be compelled to trade whatever we needed on a gold as payment basis.

Chapter 16 - Criticisms of Gold

Like anything else, gold has its critics. I am obviously pro gold, or else I wouldn't have devoted all the time of researching and writing a book about it. But I think it is only right to present some arguments made against gold. Some are of a more intimate and personal level, others are large in scope and deal with the economy as a whole. All of these criticisms have a point and on some level are valid. My goal is to present them along with how people can mitigate gold's shortcomings.

You can't earn income from gold.

True – as individual investors, you cannot earn an income by holding gold. The way to mitigate this is simply not to have all your money invested in gold. Some true gold bugs who are really die hard believers in gold really do advise people to own nothing but gold and precious metals. My view is that this would be extremely unwise. My thoughts are: have a diversified portfolio of all types of assets. Own some stocks of strong companies that pay dividends that are well covered by their net profits and cash flow. Own some bonds of highly rated issuers of corporations, municipalities, etc. As long as you don't try to chase the yield by buying too many long term bonds. Sometimes adding real estate may make sense. And into this mix , I believe it makes sense to add some gold as well (and probably some of the other precious metals as well). Professional investors and money managers sometimes use gold to help cover their "tail risk". Tail risk technically means an asset or bunch of assets as a group moving more than three standard deviations from the mean. It's not necessary to know the ins and outs of the jargon or how to calculate this out. Just be aware that money managers do use gold to basically mitigate some of their risks with other assets, and I tend to concur that it seems to make a lot of sense to add some gold in a portfolio...just in case the sh*t does hit the fan.

The point is also this: gold doesn't provide you with income, but neither do a lot of other assets. Many stocks do not pay dividends. Your house doesn't unless you own and live in a multi-family. Raw land doesn't. A rare painting by Leonardo da Vinci may be worth a fortune, but it doesn't throw off any income to the owner (unless of course you devise a clever way to exhibit it for $2 a head, the way they do for curiosities at fairs and circuses). With interest rates so low now, you barely earn any interest income by having money in the bank. This argument is not exclusive to just gold. This reasoning can be applied to all kinds of things around us. In fact, it's not even as fair with the case of gold. It seems its best use is for money. We are all evaluating it on its investment merits vs. shortcomings. But this is a very new way of looking at gold. For almost all of civilized history, it was looked upon as money – a store of value and something to be traded for stuff you want. People held gold and desired gold. Nobody "*invested*" in gold, because that didn't make any sense. Gold was money itself.

Gold is hard to store.

Because of gold's high value density, it is very easy for storage in terms of physical amount. At least it's not an issue in this regard. Nobody can honestly say that they don't have the space to store all the gold (if that were the case, chances are you're a billionaire, so congratulations).

The problem of storage does become a serious issue in terms of how to securely keep your gold. You could keep it in your home, but the critics of gold point out that this is not safe from criminals who want to burglarize your house. This is a major problem, especially if you're considering buying a significant quantity of gold. I think most people would agree that keeping anything more than a trivial amount of the physical bullion in a home safe is *not* the way to go. There are a couple of ways to consider to keep your gold safe.

First, there are ways that I *don't* recommend. One way which I already described is to keep gold in a home, either in a home safe or stashed away in hidden areas of a house. I think going this route is a very bad idea. It opens you up to break-ins by burglars that want to steal your gold. It also exposes you to a risk that if you stash your gold all over a house, you may actually forget yourself where you stashed it. Don't laugh – this kind of scenario happens more than you think. People figure they're being smart by not storing all their gold or valuables together in a central safe. They feel that if someone steals the safe, they lose 100% of their items, but if they hide small amounts all over the place, they are much safer – even if a criminal steals one stash, they haven't lost it all. While this line of thinking may be good in theory, the reality is that these people are being too smart and clever for their own good. I'll bet that more valuables have been lost this way than outright theft. One can easily imagine someone carrying out these plans and then forgetting all the places they put the valuables. Or, valuables get accidently thrown out with the garbage because either they or their family members forget or don't know that gold coins were hidden in the old spaghetti jar or whatever. Or, they die, and then the family has no idea where the valuables are. All things considered, this isn't the way to go.

The other option that I *don't* recommend sounds nice at first. Some bullion dealers will allow you to purchase your gold, then they will send it directly to a secure vault on your behalf. You end up getting paperwork that says that this depository company is holding your gold for you. I have two problems with this arrangement. The first is that you don't know, and I mean *really know*, that this is all on the up and up. The second is that assuming it is, you still have to trust this private company will take vigilante steps to secure your gold. You are placing an awful lot of trust in this company. You are essentially adding counter party risk on an asset which, in its pure form, doesn't have any. I suggest that you always take physical delivery of any gold that you buy.

The option that I do recommend is storing your physical gold in multiple safe deposit boxes at local banks. Why? There are a few reasons. Even safe deposit boxes are not guaranteed against theft. The bank essentially is doing its best efforts to protect your valuables in these boxes, but they are not immune from burglars. This is why I think it is prudent to divide up your valuables at a few different boxes located at a few different banks. It's unlikely that thieves would go after boxes anyway – they want cash currency – that's the whole point of robbing a bank. Breaking into boxes would be a slow and time consuming process that might yield the robbers a lot of paperwork and photos and lots of other family heirlooms that aren't actually worth beans. Even so, you never know. This is why you take precautions and use different boxes at different banks. I would go so far as to say that what I mean by "different banks" is not just different branches, but actually different bank companies as well. This gives you added protection just in case a particular bank goes bankrupt. You may still get what you have in your boxes eventually, but this way your access isn't limited for any amount of time to most of your valuables. How many boxes in how many banks that you need depends a lot on how big your investments are. The good news is that gold doesn't take up much space so you can rent the smallest of boxes pretty inexpensively. Using local banks is important because it gives you ready access to your gold anytime you wish. You can insure your gold against theft or loss. Think about it in terms of how difficult other physical commodities would be with storage. Investing in pork bellies anyone? What about oil or gasoline... All in all, gold is not that much of a hassle to store.

The Economy can't expand beyond the pace of mining if money is based on gold

Yes, this is technically true. In fact, the money supply can only expand by the amount of gold being discovered, mined, and brought into the system. People who are in favor of un-backed paper money use this argument to base their theories on. To them, gold is too rigid and not flexible enough. They make claims that an economy can be held back in prosperous times to the rate of mining. During bad economic times, they assert that the government needs the ability to create a lot of extra money to help the economy out of a crisis. This is what they partly blame the Great Depression on.

The opponents of gold money have to deal with some flaws in their logic as well. Giving either the government or central bankers a free hand in deciding arbitrarily how much money should be in the system is not an exact science. If it were, the Great Recession of 2009 would have been relieved easily and the economy would have been back to its glory years right away. This was in everyone's interest after all. The government and politicians wanted this. The banks wanted it. The people themselves wanted it as well. Everyone wanted the boom to start up again. And yet, with the Fed having a free hand on how much money to create (which they did in an enormous way), we went through a long, sluggish period after 2009. I think most people would agree that even now in 2016, the economy is just limping along. Our politicians and economists continue to fight about what the "true" unemployment rate really is. To listen to the gold money opponents, this wasn't supposed to have played out this way. We are left to wonder what went wrong.

Part of the problem is that the upheavals that led to both the Great Recession and the Great Depression were the result of credit and debt. The times leading up to these brutal periods were great times. Banks and creditors threw caution to the wind and just made bad decisions across the board. In both cases, all this debt was created, which nobody could actually afford to pay. In the year 2009, our paper money system was put to the test. The Fed could do whatever it wanted and not be restricted by gold. They printed massive amounts of new money to rescue the system. Did this help? Some say yes, it saved the system from going into a full blown depression like in the 1930's. But *who* exactly did this help? It didn't help We The People...It helped the *banks*. The banks were saved from not going bankrupt, which is ironic, since it was the banks themselves that were the main cause of the financial meltdown in the first place. We The People may someday suffer from all this money printing carried out by the Fed in terms of higher inflation and much more debt on our national debt. The bottom line is that using un-backed paper currency didn't live up to its promise in terms of helping people in a downturn.

So, the points gold opponents make are somewhat valid. But it's also true that under a gold standard, the central bankers and the government can't run amok and do whatever they want. Gold keeps them honest. One way to get around just mining production acting as a speed limit on the economy would be an increasing gold price. If the price of gold increased on a fairly consistent basis, this would also aid the economy expanding. There are more ways than one to keep the economy growing.

Nobody wants to carry around coins because they're heavy and not convenient

This is a major reason why the $1 bill just can't seem to be replaced with $1 coins. The government has certainly done its part in trying to convince people that the coins are a good thing. Coins certainly last a whole lot longer than paper money. People just don't want to lug around coins if they have a choice. They do have the choice, and almost everyone prefers $1 bills.

The beauty of the gold standard system is that you don't have to carry around the physical gold coins. In fact, even under a gold standard, people carried physical paper notes which were redeemable for gold and silver coin. Out in the western U.S. territories, people did carry gold and silver coin, partly because banks were a lot further apart out in those rural areas. But the people living in the eastern cities had no need to always carry the coins. They had faith in the government and knew they could get the gold anytime they wanted. It must have been great to have that level of trust in the government and banks. Even if our country went back to a gold standard, it wouldn't mean that you are required to carry gold coins everywhere you went. It simply would be that the government would be required to produce the gold if and when someone demanded it in exchange for their paper note.

Chapter 17 - Losing our Liberty

The government designated our paper money "legal tender". It says right on the paper notes in circulation "THIS NOTE IS LEGAL TENDER FOR ALL DEBTS, PUBLIC AND PRIVATE". The use of the word "private" is very important. In a nutshell, the government is forcing people to accept this paper money. Just consider – no government ever had to *force* private citizens to accept gold. This in effect strips us of our liberty to choose what type of payment we want. The real danger here is that this autocratic style can spill over into infringing on our other liberties.

Our First Amendment of Free Speech

Our right to free speech can be, and has been threatened. This happens subtly and takes the form of political correctness. So while we are still technically free to speak our minds, the politically correct crowd will ostracize us for doing this. People speaking what they believe are then frowned upon and treated as a pariah. Because of all this, many people just give in to the pressure and say whatever is politically correct. They are so afraid of the consequences that instead of taking a stand for what they believe in, they simply state what they consider "safe". The fact that the mainstream media is controlled by a handful of big corporate interests also doesn't help free speech.

The most amazing restriction on free speech comes from colleges and universities. It's amazing because these are the very institutions that pride themselves on free speech. But in reality, at most colleges and universities the strangest thing happens: this only applies when you happen to agree with the politics of the professors who are running the show. Most of the schools and professors are very liberal. So if you're liberal, then you will have their full support and guidance in orchestrating rallies and speeches. But it's a different story if you are conservative. Then these same schools and professors try to silence you. A Washington Times article does a good job describing this: "Conservatives are essentially unwelcome on the annual college commencement speaker circuit...Among the top 100 campuses in the nation, liberal speakers outnumber conservatives 6-to-1. Among the top 50, the ratio increases to 9 liberals for every one conservative. And among the elite top 10 universities, there were no conservatives invited to speak whatsoever."(1) The colleges and universities as a whole pride themselves on being above politics. It would be great if that were truly the case. The reality is that these institutions of higher learning do not always take the high road. In many cases, party politics plays out just like in every other organization.

Our Second Amendment Right to Bear Arms

The right to bear arms is expressed very clearly and plainly in the U.S. Constitution: "A well regulated Militia, being necessary to the security of a free State, the right of the people to keep and bear Arms, shall not be infringed."

With these words written into the Constitution by our founding fathers, you would think that our right to firearms would be completely safe. But the opposite is true – this right is constantly being challenged and even violated. Lets look at two cases where the Second Amendment was violated outright:

The first case is about how Washington D.C. decided a long time ago to simply ban handguns for law abiding citizens living there. "...in 2008 the U.S. Supreme Court revisited the issue in the case of District of Columbia v. Heller (07-290). The plaintiff in *Heller* challenged the constitutionality of the Washington D.C. handgun ban, a statute that had stood for 32 years. Many considered the statute the most stringent in the nation. In a 5-4 decision, the Court, meticulously detailing the history and tradition of the Second Amendment at the time of the Constitutional Convention, proclaimed that the Second Amendment established an individual right for U.S. citizens to possess firearms and struck down the D.C. handgun ban as violative of that right."(2)

The Second case involves Chicago, which also put in effect a ban on handguns. "...the Supreme Court has revitalized the Second Amendment. The Court continued to strengthen the Second Amendment through the 2010 decision in *McDonald v. City of Chicago* (08-1521). The plaintiff in *McDonald* challenged the constitutionally of the Chicago handgun ban, which prohibited handgun possession by almost all private citizens. In a 5-4 decisions, the Court, citing the intentions of the framers and ratifiers of the Fourteenth Amendment, held that the Second Amendment applies to the states.."(2).

It's great when the highest court in the nation affirms that We The People have rights. It's also very disturbing that these unconstitutional laws had to make their way to the Supreme Court to be struck down. Even more frightening is the fact that the Supreme Court decision was split 5 to 4 in *both cases*. We were all one judge's decision away from the court basically saying that it was OK to violate our constitutional right to firearms. I think most people that love liberty would agree that this was way too close for comfort.

Our Religious Liberty is increasingly under attack

Public schools put up with a lot of nonsense. Everything from kids slacking off and being disruptive to even outright bullying. There are lots of teachers that turn a blind eye to all of the crap that is going on around them (and everyone wonders why the kids in this country are not being prepared for the real world). But if a kid mentions "God" or "Jesus" then this is just unacceptable – the whole school system has a convulsion. As one example, Fox News ran a story entitled "Student punished for saying "bless you"". ..after a classmate sneezed. The student was "thrown out of class for violating the teacher's ban on the words "bless you"... "I stood up and said, 'My pastor said I have a constitutional right – 1st amendment freedom of speech,'" Kendra wrote on Facebook. "She said, 'Not in my class you don't." "The assistant principal said if I didn't want to respect my teacher's rules then maybe my pastor should teach me because my freedom (of) speech and religion does not work at their school," she wrote. (3)

This is the kind of ridiculous stuff that happens in our public schools today. At first hearing a story like this, one might laugh because of the absurdity of it. But nobody is laughing because this kind of scenario is all too common. While the whole school system – teachers and administrators are coming down hard on this one student, are all the other students behaving like model students? I doubt it. The school systems in our nation are hell bent on stamping out any type of reference to any religion. It's not only sad, its shameful.

The "In God We Trust" on our money has been the target for atheists. "The plaintiffs claimed that being forced to carry around money with the motto violates their Constitutional rights. In a nutshell, the court dismissed their complaints as petty and told them to find something more important to sue over."(4). This isn't the first time they have sued over this, and it won't be the last.

It's become commonplace for groups to sue to try to remove nativity scenes on any public lands during Christmas. How can you celebrate Christmas when you take Jesus Christ out of the celebration? The whole idea of Christmas is an acknowledgement of Jesus, not of Santa Claus or Frosty the Snowman. The politically correct crowd prefers to say "Happy Holidays" in place of "Merry Christmas".

Many people would agree that when all these types of infringements on liberty are added together, there is a preponderance of evidence that shows that our liberty is being attacked. There are people in this world that get their jollies out of making life difficult for everyone else. In a sense, when you attack one liberty, you are attacking all liberties, because our liberties are what makes us as Americans different from other people in the world. We must hold them dear and defend them against those forces who would tear them down and shred the Constitution in the process.

Chapter 18 - Fighting back has already begun

      The Gold Bullion Act of 1985 was passed which allowed the U.S. Mint to strike gold bullion coins. There was a demand for these coins which investors were buying from foreign countries, most notably the South African Krugerand. The U.S. government actually assigned them legal tender status and put denominations on the coins. For example, the U.S. mint assigns the 1 OZ coin a $50 denomination. The mint then sells them at the market price of gold plus a mintage markup. It is a curious oddity that our government, when bringing back gold coins assigns them such a low value, but yet sells them for such a high price...debasement in action.

      A businessman named Robert Kahre decided to use the United States' bullion coins to pay his workers in gold and silver coin. As the face value of a 1 OZ gold bullion coin is only $50, he paid their salary in U.S. bullion coins. The employees could then go cash in the 1 OZ gold coins for around $1,200. Because the face value of the coins are low, no tax withholding was necessary, and employees by "earning so little" really didn't owe any federal income tax. After all, the U.S. government decided to label these coins with a face value and grant them official legal tender status for the amounts listed on the coins. The IRS didn't like this very much, and prosecuted.

      "A self-made entrepreneur, Kahre, 48, paid his workers in gold and silver coin, and said they could go by the coins' face value -- rather than the much higher market value of their precious metal content -- for federal tax purposes. He did not withhold taxes from their wages, and he provided the same payroll system to 35 outside clients, which were other local businesses...Three of the four present defendants were among the nine people tried on similar charges two years ago, but no convictions resulted. In the 2007 trial, four others of the nine defendants, including Kahre's mother, were entirely acquitted. Two individuals were only partially acquitted, but dropped from the indictment that forms the basis for the trial before Ezra.(the Judge)

According to the government, Kahre and others concocted a fraudulent cash payroll "scheme" and then peddled it to other Las Vegas contractors. Defendants did not report to the IRS any payments made to workers, "either at the true amount or at the bogus amount, ... being the face value of the coin or coins," according to the indictment.The now-suspended payroll service handled about $114 million over six years, according to court records. Between 17 and 25 percent of that went to Kahre or his workers; the rest went to the 35 client businesses to pay their workers, court records show.Further, the $50 gold coins and the silver dollars Kahre used for payroll are designated by Congress as legal tender, so people are entitled to value them at their stamped denominations, he also contends. Taken at face value, each defendant's annual coin income placed him below the threshold for filing a federal tax return. Earlier cases on the question of how to value gold or silver coins have focused on collectible coins that had been pulled from circulation but still have value as property, according to the defense. Kahre used coins minted after 1985, which are allowed to circulate...Cohan described Kahre's payroll system as a "boycott of the Federal Reserve." But when the lawyer attempted to elaborate on Kahre's view that the nation has debased its paper currency by abandoning its former gold standard, Ezra added, "We're not here to convince the jury that the ... (U.S.) monetary system belongs to an international cabal."(1)

It appears what happened is that with the first trial, he got away with this, but this proves that once someone starts doing this on a large scale, the IRS will go after you. They were not about to let it go. He was convicted in a 2009 trial. "Kahre was convicted in 2009 of conspiracy to defraud the Internal Revenue Service, tax evasion and hiding assets. But his real crime was something far more serious in the eyes of the IRS and federal prosecutors. Kahre paid his employees as independent contractors rather than salaried employees and he paid them in gold and silver coin. By doing so, he brought unwelcome attention to the ongoing official debasement of our money supply. This action is what brought the full might of the federal government crashing down upon him."(2)

Here is another example. In a..."town of about 33,000 is also the home of Late's, a small-town diner just a few hundred yards from Lake Michigan and still lined with a long, winding counter and spinning stools. And there, placed high on the south wall near the ceiling, the restaurant is trying something new to both attract customers and secure its future: It's offering a huge discount if customers pay with silver change minted before 1965. How big? How about a hamburger for 12 cents, or 10 of them for $1. Like fries? 10 cents. Chicken? 100 pieces for $4.55. And you better believe in a state where fish fries on Fridays are as common as Packers games on Sundays you can nab a Perch sandwich for 20 cents... With the value of the dollar going down, we think the price of silver – the value of silver – is going up," Todd Tikalsky, the restaurant's manager who's been there for 27 years, told TheBlaze during an interview at the restaurant. Tikalsky, with his tennis shoes and a classic, white cooking apron, understands business: He has an accounting degree and moonlights as a tax preparer during the spring. As an accountant, he and the restaurant's owner, Karl Birkenstock, understand that silver change minted before 1965 is worth more than just its face value. That's because the coins at that time were actually made with silver.(3)

This is not just a Conservative issue. Republican Congressman Ron Paul has gone after the Federal Reserve during his time in Congress. But some very liberal Democrats have gone after the big banks as well. As these words are being written, Senator Bernie Sanders of Vermont is running against Secretary Hillary Clinton for the Democratic Presidential nomination. Senator Sanders ("Bernie" as he is known) is confronting the issues of how the whole economic system is rigged. Bernie has gone so far as to proclaim that "The business model of Wall Street is fraud" on MSNBC's primary debate.

Bernie has gone after Hillary Clinton as being the ultimate insider. One major issue has been Hillary Clinton's speeches to Goldman Sachs that netted her more than half a million dollars. "In 2013 alone, Clinton made $675,000 after giving three speeches to Goldman Sachs for $225,000 a pop"(4). Bernie has been calling for Hillary to release the transcripts of what she said at those speeches to Goldman Sachs. He has been on all the news networks saying how those speeches must have been pretty amazing speeches for the investment bank to pay over $200,000 for each one.

Of course, we all know that it's really not what she said at those speeches that is the real issue here. No, there's something far worse at play. We all know that those insanely high speaking fees boil down to nothing more than bribes. Because we all know in our hearts that no "speech" can be worth this astronomical amount of money. This is how Goldman Sachs and other large banks buy access. Clinton, for her part has tried to defend what she did as "normal". The awful reality is that Goldman Sachs effectively bought themselves a puppet. If Hillary wins, that's great for them – because they own her. Anything that comes up that they don't like, and you can be assured that the CEO will reach out to Clinton and let his views be known. Clinton has argued the point that this money does not influence her, just as it has not influenced President Obama. The flaw in what she says is this: any rational person knows that it does. It has too. Bernie has called all of this part of the "Corrupt campaign finance system" that he rails against.

After all, this is the same Goldman Sachs that paid a $5.1 billion dollar fine for its role in toxic mortgages. These are the mortgages that hurt both homeowners and hurt investors who thought they were investing in something safe for their retirement funds. These are real people who got hurt as a result of the investment bank's greed. This is also the same Goldman Sachs that owns a piece of the Federal Reserve System – the privately owned cartel that has the awesome power to print money and set interest rates. The same Goldman Sachs whose executives have not been prosecuted for their deeds. Bernie has been asking how a bank can pay a $5 billion fine, but yet the executives escape not only prison sentences, but even an attempt at prosecution? Where is the justice? Could it be that it's somehow related to the lavish contributions that they make to politicians? Bernie Sanders contrasts this situation to people using marijuana getting prosecuted and then having a criminal record. Many would agree that the same thing happens with those Americans who used legal tender gold coins to pay their employees. The government, through the IRS, went after them with a vengeance, and did not stop until they were imprisoned. You would think that as a "free people" we have a right to enter into any payment an employer and employee agree to. These gold transactions did not hurt anyone. But the heads of Goldman Sachs along with other big banks that contributed to the financial mess that ruined people's lives received no prison time.

Cracks in our monetary system have already begun to show. People are starting to figure out that our paper "money" isn't worth as much as "real money". This Diner owner figured it out. The business owner who tried to pay his employees in gold bullion figured it out and paid for his creativity with his liberty being stripped away. When things start falling apart, the government needs to rely on force to stop this. Otherwise, everyone would start doing it. But this is how change happens – with isolated incidents here and there. The government, at the behest of the big banks who are pulling the strings, go after these people to set an example. Or, simply ignore people who dissent on a small scale, and laugh them off as "quacks". But when the anti-bank movement grows into something too big, then politicians can't fight everyone. Not if they want to keep their job. Politicians then must succumb to the will of the people. If they don't, new politicians will run on an anti-bank platform and be elected to take their place. It doesn't matter Republican or Democrat. Conservative or Liberal. The masses can see what is happening. In our information age, it is becoming harder and harder for the big banking cartel to cover up their unholy alliance with the government.

Some of the people have already figured out that our paper money is fake and is on shaky ground and have reacted by looking for an alternative. Some of these individuals have gravitated toward different electronic currencies. These currencies are not national currencies issued by other nations (this wouldn't help much since no nation is currently backing their currency with gold at the present time). Instead these currencies are more or less private concerns. They come in two general flavors: digital gold currencies and cryptocurrency.

The idea of having a digital gold currency attracted some interest from people. The idea was pretty simple – have an electronic currency that was backed by gold held in a vault someplace. People could pay in grams or fractions of an ounce of gold. In essence, these private companies were attempting to mimic what the dollar used to be, only on an online type basis. The U.S. government didn't let all this stand. They eventually went after companies such as e-gold and charged them with operating as an illegal and unlicensed money transfer business. They effectively closed down these types of businesses.

The other type of electronic currency is cryptocurrency based on computer programs. The best known is called Bitcoin. It uses cryptography which is computer programs to control money supply. People use special computer programs to "mine" for Bitcoins. This idea had a lot of news coverage for a while because the "value" of a Bitcoin fluctuated so wildly. The Independent Review featured Bitcoin on its cover and stated "As with any unprecedented innovation bold claims are made for it. The boldest, perhaps, is the claim that cryptocurrency in general or Bitcoin in particular can or will supplant the current international regime of central-bank-issued monies."(17)

I don't endorse either of these types of currencies. They all suffer from many inherent flaws. The gold currency idea presents a lot of risk – you are totally trusting that this gold really exists in the first place. And that you won't be cheated on purpose. One can only imagine all the ways this can go wrong. As for Bitcoin, it suffers from the same issues. We have a case that happened back in 2010 where some computer savvy person(s) found a weakness in Bitcoin's software and used this to take advantage of the system. Consider this: nobody even knows who created Bitcoin in the first place. All anyone knows is that "Satoshi Nakamoto" was the creator but nobody knows who or what this is – a person going by this fake name, a group of people, an organization of some type? It's anyone's guess. Would you feel comfortable venturing into all these unknowns? I don't.

All this electronic "currency" popping up shows that people are dissatisfied with the dollar and all the paper money out there. I get it. Some people are on to the false promises of currency backed by no assets. One of the benefits of Bitcoin is that it is decentralized – not controlled by any central bank. People are reaching for alternatives to unbacked paper currency. The present condition of our dollar and of all the other national currencies is that they are essentially fake and worthless. The point that people looking to this virtual currency don't seem to understand is that they are no more real than the paper currency in our wallets. Maybe even less so, since they are one computer crash or hack job away from annihilation. The people should take a look at all of this and understand that the world already has the perfect alternative to worthless paper currency – it's called gold (or perhaps silver). There is no need to play this game of dealing with computerized currency nonsense. (Author's note: for fans of Bitcoin or stuff like it, I'm sorry. I understand your motivation but I don't get your answer. And in fair disclosure, I'm not at all a techie or whatever the lingo is for savvy high tech type people. Maybe you're on to something, but it's not for me, and I can't recommend any of it). Either way, these tech savvy people are fighting back by putting their faith in another type of currency.

For those who think fighting back has no chance of winning, just look at history. There are success stories of Americans fighting a central bank here in the U.S. and winning.

The first time a central bank was created goes far back in U.S. history. This bank was called The Bank of North America., chartered in 1781 by Congressman Robert Morris. "The Bank of North America was modeled closely after the Bank of England. Following the practice of fractional reserve, it was allowed to issue paper promissory notes in excess of actual deposits, but, since some gold and silver had to be held in the vault, there were definite limits to how far that process could go. Bank notes were not forced on the people as legal tender for all debts, public and private, but the government did agree to accept them at their face value in payment of all taxes and duties, which made them as good as gold for that specific purpose. Furthermore, unlike the central banks of today, the Bank of North America was not given the power to directly issue the nation's money...The Bank of North America was fraudulent from the very start. The charter required that private investors provide $400,000 for the initial subscription...when Morris was unable to raise that money...he took the gold that had been lent to the United States from France and had it deposited in the Bank. Then, using this as a fractional-reserve base, he simply created the money that was needed for the subscription and lent it to himself and his associates...It must be remembered that the war was still in progress when the charter was issued."(5). "Despite the monopoly privileges conferred upon the Bank of North America and its nominal redeemability in specie, the market's lack of confidence in the inflated notes led to their depreciation outside the Bank's home base in Philadelphia...By the end of 1783...the first experiment with a central bank in the United States had ended."(6). Due to the circumstances,of fighting the Revolutionary War, most of us can understand the need to perform this trickery at the time. The Congress had the good sense to end this bank only a couple of years after its founding.

The second time a central bank in the U.S. came into existence was in 1791. This effort was led by Alexander Hamilton, and was called the (First) Bank of the United States. Thomas Jefferson opposed this as he believed this was unconstitutional. "Hamilton, on the other hand, argued that debt was a good thing, if kept within reason, and that the nation needed more money in circulation to keep up with expanding commerce...in 1791, Congress granted a twenty-year charter to the Bank of the United States...it was almost an exact replica of the previous Bank of North America...The new Bank of the United States was to have eighty per cent of its capital provided by private investors with the federal government putting up only twenty per cent."(7)

"Who were these private investors? Their names do not appear in the published literature, but we can be certain they included the Congressmen and Senators-and their associates-who engineered the charter. But there is an interesting line ..."foreigners could own shares but not vote them"(8)...The blunt reality is that the Rothschild banking dynasty in Europe was the dominant force, both financially and politically, in the formation of the Bank of the United States. Biographer, Derek Wilson, explains: "Over the years since N.M. (Rothschild), the Manchester textile manufacturer, had bought cotton from the Southern states, Rothschilds had developed heavy American commitments. Nathan...had made loans to various states of the Union, had been, for a time, the official European banker for the U.S. government and was a pledged supporter of the Bank of the United States".(9). Gustavus Myers, in his History of the Great American Fortunes, is more pointed. He says: "Under the surface, the Rothschilds long had powerful influence in dictating American financial laws. The law records show that they were the power in the old Bank of the United States"(10). The Rothschilds, therefore, were not merely investors nor just an important power. They were the power behind the Bank of the United States!"(11).

The Bank of the United States was opposed by two forces: The first were the "Jeffersonians...they believed it was unconstitutional and because they wanted a monetary system based only upon gold and silver coin...the other group was made up of the wildcatters, the land speculators, and the empire-building industrialists. They opposed the Bank because they wanted a monetary system with no restraints at all, not even those associated with fractional reserve...Congress...was deadlocked...the bill for charter renewal had been defeated by *one* vote in the House and *one* vote, cast by Vice-President George Clinton to break the tie, in the Senate. And so on January 24, 1811, the Bank of the United States closed its doors"(12). It's amazing that the gridlock of Congress actually ended up being the death blow to the Central Bank. Congress actually helped We The People by being so screwed up! Ominously, Nathan Rothschild lashed out: "Either the application for renewal of the Charter is granted", he is said to have threatened, "or, the United States will find itself in a most disastrous war." When the charter was not granted, the United States did find itself in another war with England, the War of 1812".(15). Most would agree that this shows the power the Rothschilds had and surely they *at least* helped guide England to war with the U.S., if not outright forced it.

The third central bank of the U.S. was The Second Bank of the United States that came into existence after the War of 1812 in1816 with a twenty year charter. "In every respect the new bank was a carbon copy of the old, with one minor exception. Congress unashamedly extracted from the private investors what amounted to nothing less than a bribe in the form of $1.5 million...the bankers were glad to pay the fee, not only because it was a modest price for such a profitable enterprise, but also because, as before, they received an immediate government deposit of one-fifth the total capitalization which then was used as the base for manufacturing much of the remaining startup capital...Another important continuity between the old and new Bank was the concentration of foreign investment. In fact, the largest single block of stock in the new Bank, about one-third in all, was held by this group...The Second Bank of the United States was rooted as deeply in Britain as it was in America"(13).

This didn't sit well with President Andrew Jackson. "...it was well known that Baron James de Rothschild of Paris was the principal investor in this central bank."(16)When the charter was attempted to be renewed in 1832, four years earlier than expiration, he vetoed it. "The Bank's charter expired in 1836"(14).

The fourth central bank in the U.S. is the Federal Reserve, which came into existence in 1913. As "the Fed" as its commonly called, is covered extensively in another chapter, it will not be explored in detail here. The only thing worth saying is that We The People are all currently living with this central bank calling the shots.

It is possible to get rid of an unconstitutional central bank. It has been done three times in U.S. history. It will be harder this time, mainly because the current central bank has now been allowed to exist just over 100 years instead of the 20 years as in the past. The Fed has used this time to its advantage. It has very effectively burnished its image, and been successful at making many citizens believe they are somehow part of the U.S. government. They are not. The Fed is just as private as the other incarnations before. Amazingly, it was also founded with the Rothschild family pulling the strings in 1913, just as they did in 1816 and 1791. The Rothschild family was certainly persistent if nothing else.

This is all somewhat balanced by one advantage We The People have now that never existed before: better communication. People today are more informed than ever before. And I'm not just talking about what the biased media spoon feeds us. With the Internet, we all have the power. The power to think for ourselves and the ability to communicate our thoughts to many others over a huge distance. This is a game changer. Each and every one of us now has the ability to become a broadcaster of ideas and information. Because of the ready availability of news and communication, people are far less gullible today. They are more cynical and distrusting of our leaders and institutions. It is far harder for the big banking interests to hide their agendas and influence politicians without us all knowing about it. People take information with a grain of salt. They don't take things at face value anymore. This is all a good thing. A more informed populace will help as We The People take back control of our country.

Chapter 19 - How do I see all this playing out in the future?

I'll start by saying that nobody has a crystal ball. Nobody. The best that we all have is to look at the past. We do have history to study. One of the best ways to look into the future is to see how events played out in the past and try to get a read on how the present condition will change in the future. Here is my take:

Many predict that Social Security and Medicare will go bankrupt, and the people – especially the younger folks, who are paying into the system will never get the benefits promised them. I do not share this view, but am still concerned for different reasons. People have this idea that these two programs literally have a "trust fund" that is actually accumulating money you are forced to contribute and that this money is put aside for you for when you're old and gray. Nothing can be further from reality. The money you pay out of your paycheck now is simply transferred to those who are retired and drawing benefits. This system worked quite well when there were 8 people supporting 1 retiree. It doesn't work nearly as well if there are only 2 working people supporting every retiree. This is at the root of the problem. It shows up in nightmare scenarios from groups like the AARP. Long term, this is not sustainable. Something will have to give.

My thought is that at some point, the government will end up raising the age in which you are allowed to receive benefits. As mentioned, I do not believe that the government will reneg on their promises to pay. This would be too politically dangerous for whoever our politicians happen to be. Instead, I think it will play out by the government turning to the Fed and pushing them to simply create more money out of thin air to pay all the people.

So things will be OK then, right? Wrong. I believe the government will pay out the numerical value it owes you under these programs. But, this tells us nothing about the *value* of that money. By printing massive amounts of money out of thin air, the process lowers the value of all money, otherwise known as inflation. So, as young people, when you look at a statement and see that in 30 years you will get say $1,000 per month – what if the money falls so much that by then, a loaf of bread costs $100, and eggs cost $200? You'll get the government money, and it would barely cover the cost of 1 trip to a quicky mart. My example is extreme here to show you a point. I do think the government will technically honor the program, but they will do so *in dollars, not in value.*

Middle class and working class folks tend to gravitate to bonds because they perceive them as being safe. Unfortunately, they are not safe at all. In particular, the long term bonds are risky. Highly rated bonds may be safe in terms of getting your original principal back, but in many years, it may not be worth anything close to what it is now.

I can pretty much guarantee three things: 1. Death 2. Taxes. 3.The U.S. dollar continuing to fall in value. How can I be so sure of this last one? I think all three are inevitable, unless something truly radical happens. If humanity suddenly discovers the fountain of youth or a medicine that is the equivalent of that, then, I concede, that would be a game changer. There will always be a tax levied by someone. Even if you move to a state with no personal income tax, there will always be the federal tax to pay. If the U.S. federal government goes bust and ceases to exist, then local taxes will have to be paid. Basically, we pay for government no matter what. Unless complete anarchy happens, I don't ever see this changing. The dollar declining – why is this so inevitable? Just look at history...what did a dollar buy you 50 years ago? What can it buy you now? The only thing that can reverse this slide in the dollar's purchasing power is to change the system – that would be a game changer.

How could the system be changed?

The first thing most people think of as a solution is for our government to begin minting money in gold and silver bullion; and to start printing paper money that is backed by these precious metals. This idea is far too simplistic. It would never work. The reason is something called "Gresham's Law" which states "When a government overvalues one type of money and undervalues another, the undervalued money will leave the country or disappear from circulation into hoards, while the overvalued money will flood into circulation". (1) You can't just start pumping good money into the economy and expect it to replace the bad money. It won't happen. The good money backed by gold and silver will simply be hoarded. The bad money – in our case, the un-backed U.S. dollars will be the circulating currency because they would be the grossly overvalued money. The undervalued money – gold and silver – people hold dear, and will want to hold onto. So what we have is this: Bad money quickly drives out good money, but good money can never drive out bad money. So the thought of keeping all the paper money out there "as is" and just starting to make good, solid money from now on is not feasible – they will not circulate together.

We could go back to a system where the U.S. dollar is backed by gold. Naysayers will point out that this is impossible because of the vast amounts of dollars outstanding. They will say that there is simply not enough gold in existence to cover all of the outstanding dollars. They are correct. But, it depends on what price for gold we are using. It would be unthinkable to envision going back to the old level where a gold coin represented gold at about $20 or about $35 per ounce. That's not going to happen with the dollars now in existence. The key is the price of gold – if set high enough, it could back the U.S. currency. There are two ways I see that the U.S. can go back to a sound monetary system backed by gold.

The first way is to leave the dollars that exist intact, but declare them to be now backed by gold. The U.S. mint could coin gold coins with a very high dollar denomination. For an extreme example, as of this writing, an ounce of gold is around $1,150 per ounce. If the U.S. government ordered the mint to produce a one ounce gold coin, it could be struck with a face value of $50,000. Why on earth would they value it so highly? Because then the face value would far exceed the metal value. This is a key to understanding the concept: If the value of the underlying gold or other precious metal is higher than the face value, then the coins will not circulate, they will be hoarded instead, and maybe melted down for other uses such as jewlry, etc. By placing a denomination far higher than what the metal is trading for, the coins are worth more being used as currency rather than being hoarded. In this extreme case I put forward, where a one ounce gold coin is valued at $50,000, other denominations would follow this same valuation. So a ½ ounce gold coin would carry a denomination of $25,000, a 1/10 th ounce gold coin would carry a face value of $5,000, etc. It basically would be another way of saying that a dollar is worth X amount of gold (in the $50,000/ounce scenario, a dollar would represent 0.00002 ounces of gold). This would give our money at least *some* gold backing which is better than none. In order to make this situation work, the government would be wise to get rid of the Federal Reserve, as we can't just keep printing money out of thin air. In fact the government, through the U.S. Treasury and U.S. Mint, would manage the nation's monetary supply, and they would have to be very careful to not print too many dollars. Gold backing would keep them honest,

The second way is to basically start over with a new currency altogether. The current dollars would become exchangeable on some rate with the new currency. (This is how the Weimer Republic eventually changed over their system that was failing – in the end, one trillion German marks bought you 1 German Reichsmark). In this scenario, x number of dollars would buy you one – let's call them "New Dollar'. The United States has never done this – a dollar coin minted in the 1800's is still legal tender even today (even though it is worth considerably more to coin collectors and precious metal investors). By always keeping the old money valid, the U.S. government gets to showcase the fiction of how "stable" our money is (even though the reality is the purchasing power has not been at all stable). (Some big and stable countries do this routinely with every change of design of their currency – they're not changing their whole system, but the idea is to undermine counterfeiters. People are given a window in which you can exchange your old paper notes for new ones, usually on a one for one basis.). Other countries have used this method to fix their monetary system. When the currency gets too screwed up, the leaders just shrug their shoulders and tell people how the old money is now worthless, and we are using this new currency instead. It seems like a neat trick, and it would be the easier way of the two. It's also very third-world...this is what the dictators do in banana republics. The problem is obvious, all the citizens that have worked and saved all their lives are told "too bad". If the U.S. government went this way, then hopefully they will have learned their lesson and put in a sound, gold backed currency, and dumped the Federal Reserve to prevent overprinting of the money going forward.

I do believe that at some point, the U.S. dollar will continue getting so weak, it will be near worthless. This may not be for a long time. I think (and hope) that in the short and medium term, the dollar just keeps slowly losing its value, because that's really the best we can hope for. I don't think we will experience an abrupt, rapid decline in the dollar (hyperinflation) any time soon (But be aware that the German people in the 1910's and 1920's didn't expect that to happen, either – but it did). But in the long term sense, the dollar, as it's currently constructed, will be worth what all paper is worth – nothing.

When this is happening, people will become painfully aware of how they have been deceived. Inflation turns to hyperinflation, which is really the last period and twilight before the outright collapse of a currency and a government. People will be rioting in the streets. They will have nothing to lose – everyone's savings will be wiped out. The government will most likely rely upon the increasingly frequent use of military style police, and even the military itself to keep order and maintain their control. Eventually the pressure of the people demanding change will result in an all out revolution. This is what I see happening when we arrive at the death of the U.S. dollar as we know it. It won't be a nice meeting with government officials and bankers sipping coffee looking at computer screens. It will be a violent and bloody struggle, born of the people's misery. The best we can hope for is that this is a long way off into the future. The scariest part...nobody knows, until this is already upon us.

Given these ideas, some smart people in the banking world and government are trying to figure out ways to avoid such a dollar disaster, right? The U.S. government is doing what all governments have always done. They are focusing not on fixing the underlying problem, but on tricks to ensure their survival

Giving "Bread and Circus" is not a new idea. It basically means that as long as people are fed and entertained, things are OK. The people are too distracted to notice what the government is up to. In ancient Rome, Roman citizens were given free bread and circus (entertainment of the day). This was a way politicians bought their votes.

These practices are still being used by the U.S. today. Take a look at the Food Stamp programs across the country. These food stamps can be used to buy chips and dip. The same people using them then pay cash for their beer and liquor before getting in their late model car. Do Food Stamps really prevent hunger in the U.S? I'm sure in some cases they do. I am also sure that in other cases it doesn't and is used more as a political tool - politicians are basically bribing the people for support come election day. This isn't about shaming people. It is about shaming the system. The system is creating dependence of the people on the government. The people who try to rise up and work more find their benefits cut by the degree they increase their earnings. This creates a disincentive for people to be industrious. The end result is that it enables people not to starve but also ensures that they never can get ahead. It actually helps to keep people poor under the guise of helping them.

Circus or "entertainment" is used even more extensively. Lots of people like playing or watching sports (myself included). But what has happened to the U.S. over the last 50 years or so? As a nation, we have a radical and unhealthy fixation on sports. Now parents are mislead into thinking they are raising the next Tom Brady or Mickey Mantle. They are deluding themselves, and this translates the wrong message to their kids. It is just unrealistic. Sports has always enjoyed a following and is part of the American way of life. The difference is that way back, it was correctly seen as recreation. Today, kids neglect real schoolwork, which is why our nation is consistently falling behind other countries in academics. Kids become painfully aware of the situation when they get to the college level. What they find is that all too often it is not the American kids at the head of the class. I saw this firsthand at the pharmacy college I attended. The foreign students who come to the U.S. to study take academics very seriously. They are the ones who showcase that they have the brains, the preparation, and most importantly, the discipline to persevere and succeed. In my own college graduating class, over half the class never made it to actually receive their degree. The attrition rate was atrocious, but most of the men and women not cutting it were the American students. Rarely did a foreigner not make it, despite their disadvantage of knowing English as their second or third language and being unfamiliar with the culture.

People defend sports by saying that it teaches team building. I agree – it does. That works out great if we were living in a communist or socialist country. It's useful, but not *that* useful. American life is not a team sport. You may have a thousand Facebook virtual friends, but other than your family, you have no team in life. You have to stand on your own two feet and make it. Rugged, tough individualism. Pulling yourself up by the bootstraps is the American way of life.

As society falls apart, government uses this Bread and Circus routine to its advantage to divert our attention away from a failing economy. War is often used when nations are desperate to divert attention from their failings (The U.S. has been in an almost continuous war over the past decade). Meanwhile, the value of the dollar is falling. Faith in America is falling. With our national debt of $19 Trillion and entitlement program obligations such as Social Security, Medicare, and pensions standing at a multiple of this figure, we are all in the same boat – and that boat is headed for a cliff.

Don't underestimate the power of the big banks that want the dollar to constantly decline in value. We have been conditioned to accept inflation as normal. We expect things to cost more every year. We look back into the past and marvel at how "cheap" things were 20, 30, 80 years ago. Of course, the goods weren't cheap at all, it was the dollar that was so much stronger back then. The dollar has become cheapened over time due to inflation. It's interesting when you go back even further and compare say 1850 to 1900, you find that prices hadn't changed at all. That's because with a gold-backed dollar, inflation was basically non-existent. I don't see the system changing any time soon. At least not until the value of the dollar declines so much so fast that there are literally riots in the streets to do something about it. Until that day comes, I think what we'll see is the slow, insidious drop in the value of the dollar that we have all grown accustomed to. The present system, as it's set up, is just too easy to keep going for those in charge. A complete overhaul of the monetary system would be just too big and too difficult for any politician to truly deal with. Instead, they will go along having the Fed print ever more money, while giving their re-election speeches promising better days ahead. So, with all this said, what can we do to protect ourselves?

Chapter 20 - How can the Working Class and Middle Class protect themselves?

As this is a book about the merits of gold, I do support the idea of holding *some* gold. How much is an individual choice. I would not advocate just buying up all the gold you can get, and excluding everything else. A weakness of gold and other metals is that it provides no income for you. While this strategy *could* work out, and gold has done much better than dollars as far as holding value, we don't know the future. Anybody that claims to, well, they're either lying or crazy (and if they really insist they can predict the future, you should tell them to go and buy a lottery ticket...and run the other way!). I would advocate looking at your total portfolio, and adding some gold to balance out the risks that your other asset classes leave you exposed to. In addition to gold, a smaller amount of other precious metals such as Silver and platinum, and maybe even palladium may round out your portfolio nicely.

Stay away from buying a lot of long-term bonds. I know a lot of people believe in bonds being safer than anything else. The credit rating agency grades do NOT take future inflation into account. So while AAA or AA bonds may indeed be signs of a strong government/municipality/corporation, the strength is simply measuring the likelihood of the issuer paying you back your principal at the end of the term, as well as paying the interest payments along the way. But what good will that lump sum principal be to you, if the money has lost most of its purchasing power by the time you receive it back? In that case, you may get all your money back and received all the interest as promised, and still come out a loser. I know why people buy longer term bonds. It's because the longer the expiration date of the bonds, the more interest those bonds will pay. In this yield starved environment (thanks again to the Fed) We The People want and need the yield. I would not advocate chasing this extra yield. If you're intent on buying long term bonds, I would commit only a minimal amount of a portfolio to this. I think a safer option for bond buyers is to buy short term bonds that mature at most in a few years. If these historically low rates go up, you will have your initial principal back that you can re-invest at a higher rate of interest. I think the strategy of planning a bond ladder is a good one so long as you're not going too far out in terms of maturity date.

If you have mortgage debt on your home, I think a fixed rate 30 year mortgage makes a lot of sense. It will give you peace of mind knowing your payment will always be the same. Just think – if the dollar suddenly collapses into anything near hyperinflation, you could make out like a bandit! If you had bought any asset that goes up in value under these circumstances, such as gold, you might well be able to cash in those assets and be free of any debt on your home. With a little planning, you will know that you have put yourself in a position the same as those rich industrial owners enjoyed back in the Weimer Republic of Germany did, and be able to wipe all your debts clean. I'm not saying it will happen, probably not, but if you position yourself in this manner, you might, just *might*, enjoy a windfall beyond your wildest dreams.

I won't go so far as to say that stocks in general would do well in a situation where the dollar is falling fast, and inflation is rampant. But I do believe that certain types of stocks may do OK. I'm thinking of companies that sell consumer staples – things that people need to buy. Ideally, a financially strong company that sells low priced products that people use up quickly and need to buy more of. What Warren Buffett would refer to as "wide moat" companies because of their strong competitive position. These types of companies operate maybe not with a monopoly, as commonly described, but with a sort of "consumer monopoly" working in their favor. Usually they enjoy strong brand names that help sell their products. Industries that you tend to find these companies: food, beverage, candy, soap, tobacco, and others.

To give an example, the Coca-Cola Company is a big holding of Warren Buffett's Berkshire Hathaway. This company may fit the criteria. If the company is selling a Coke for $1 and then inflation starts to get out of hand, the firm can start charging $2 for a coke a lot easier than other companies. Compare this against the automobile industry. If General Motors is selling a pickup truck for $40,000, and inflation ramps up, can GM double the price and start selling the pickup for $80,000? Probably not without losing most of their sales. The automotive industry is more "cyclical" – meaning it depends on the cycle of the economy. Think about a Caribbean cruise that has become a middle class/working class vacation mainstay. When the economy is good, spending $3,500 for a cruise might tempt us to book a cruise with Carnival or Royal Caribbean. If inflation makes the dollar decline enough, will people be willing to spend $7,000 on that cruise – at a time when surely, people are already reeling from an economy that has taken a bad turn downward? I doubt it.

I'm obviously oversimplifying things here to drive home a point. There is so much more to investing decisions. But it is beyond the scope of this book. To go into all the details, I would have to write a complete book just talking about different metrics and philosophies. I want to give you a frame of mind as a starting off point when looking at the world. If you are mentally cognizant of the country and world as it is now with un-backed currency that is always falling in value, you may see things in a different light.

Notice how I did not mention Investment Real Estate right at the beginning of this chapter. This was on purpose. Real Estate has a good record of keeping up with inflation. Real estate has a tendency to rise in price to compensate for the weaker dollars. It also has the ability to generate rental income for you. On the surface, it would seem to be the perfect fit – it has gold's advantages, but none of its weaknesses, right? Well, kind of. Investment real estate has two major drawbacks. First is it requires you to go into debt to buy it (unless you're already super rich, and in this case, you probably don't care about this chapter anyway). There are different opinions on debt. Some of these financial gurus try to tell you how there is good debt versus bad debt. Maybe that's true ...I understand what they are driving at, but in my mind debt is bad – all debt. The second major disadvantage is that real estate takes money to operate. I've owned rental properties – everything from single families to duplexes to apartment buildings. One thing I can tell you is that promoters of real estate often gloss over this second point. The first expense is the monthly mortgage payment. Lets say you did own the property free and clear of any mortgage. It still takes money. There are real estate taxes which can be significant. The property needs to be insured, the electric bill, water bill, repairs. Yes – repairs. If you think that renters will treat your property with kid gloves, then you're kidding yourself. People make the mistake of not factoring in a vacancy percentage in figuring their cash flow calculations. If I had a dollar every time I heard a realtor say that in such and such neighborhood vacancy won't be a problem...you get the picture. I'm not trying to scare people away from being a landlord. I've owned properties that have been great – they have provided me positive cash flow income every month. I have also had my share of loser properties. A property can be a good investment if acquired at the right price, in the right location, at the right time.

Some enterprising people looking for an edge may be thinking something I want to dispel altogether. They might be thinking along the line "Since the dollar is doomed to fall and ultimately fail, then I'll spend money freely – buy a great big house to live in, buy expensive luxury cars, run up my credit cards to have vacations to exotic destinations and enjoy lavish restaurant meals. And I'll be OK – because I'll just pay it all off when hyperinflation hits and I can pay it all off easy." Well – NO! Life doesn't work out that way. It is always possible that the inflation and dollar weakening I see won't happen at all (I think it will at some point, but what happens if that point is so far in the future that it's beyond our lives?). This way off thinking is wrong and dangerous because it is only fixed rate, long term debt I am talking about. Your home is the only item that a bank will loan you money at a low enough fixed rate for decades in the future. Car loans are at most 5 or 6 years. Credit cards will jack up your interest rate almost overnight. Don't play this game!

Chapter 21 - Investing in gold the right way

Assuming that you have made the decision to add some gold to your portfolio, there has never been a time when there are so many options to consider. This is both a blessing and a curse. I actually think it is all a blessing, so long as you do enough research so you don't get ripped off. You want to be sure you are getting what you want and what you paid for.

Lets look at physical gold first. This is the most straightforward way to own gold. You buy it, and you can hold it, touch it, feel it. There are many subcategories within the physical ownership realm. Historic gold coins, modern bullion coins, gold bars.

When talking about historic gold coins, the old American gold is typically referred to as "Pre '33" This is in reference to 1933 – the last year gold coins were minted by the U.S. meant for circulation as money. The coins were based on the idea of an "Eagle". The eagle coin was a $10 gold coin. The reason was simple – for many years, the $10 gold coin was the highest denomination coin minted. Lesser amounts were based on this. The $5 gold coin was/is referred to as a "half eagle" (half the face value and half the gold as an eagle). The $2.50 gold coin a "quarter eagle" (quarter the denomination, and quarter the gold content of an eagle). Years later, in 1850, the $20 gold coin was introduced as a result of the 1849 California gold strike. This $20 gold coin is known as a "double eagle" as it not only has double the denomination, but also double the gold content as an eagle. The US Mint also produced tiny $1 coins as well as much rarer denominations such as $3 and $4 coins.

All of these coins are 90% gold between the years listed (there were gold coins minted before the years in parenthesis on the $2.50, $5.00, and $10 denominations which had a slightly higher gold percentage, but these older coins are rare and trade as collectibles with much higher prices than their gold value. I have excluded these very old coins since they would not be relevant to gold buyers. In fact, even the years listed below do not trade all the same. Some particular years are extremely rare and their prices are much higher. A lot of the oldest coins in these ranges sell for significant premiums. Remember, we are only looking at what is called "common date" in these categories" The data: (1)

$2.50 Gold coin "quarter eagle" (years 1840-1929)

Weight = 4.1800 grams

Actual Gold Weight = 0.1209 OZ

Size = 18mm

$5.00 Gold coin "half eagle" (years 1839-1929)

Weight = 8.3590 grams

Actual Gold Weight = 0.2419 OZ

Size = 21.6mm

$10 Gold coin "eagle" (years 1838 -1933)

Weight = 16.7180 grams

Actual Gold Weight = 0.4837 OZ

Size = 27mm

$20 Gold coin "double eagle" (years 1850-1933)

Weight = 33.4360 grams

Actual Gold Weight = 0.9675 OZ

Size = 34mm

Notice that the size of the coin does not double in millimeters (mm) from each denomination. This is due to the fact that the larger the denomination, the thickness of the coins increase. The weight is the total weight of the coin if you were to put it on a gram scale. However, remember that these coins are only 90% gold, not 100% gold. That's because these coins were minted with the intent of them being circulating money to be used in commerce. The other 10% of the composition is copper, to make the coins harder and not wear out as fast.

Weights are based on 31.1035 grams per *troy* ounce. This always confuses people as the commercial (or avoirdupois) ounce is more commonly used and has less grams per ounce. Gold always uses the TROY ounce.

As an example, let's look at the $20 gold double eagle. When you pick one of these coins up and weigh it, they weigh 33.4360 grams (these are *heavy* coins!). The coin weighs more than one ounce (31.1035 grams)! People who are not familiar with how this works sometimes think it has more gold than it does. Remember, the coin is only 90% gold. So the amount of gold it contains is less than an ounce at 0.9675 OZ. Another way to look at this is to say it has 96.75% of an ounce of pure gold in a coin.

At one time, these pre '33 coins were the only option available Americans had to legally own and invest in gold bullion. The reason is that when the government confiscated gold in 1933, there was an exemption for holding a small number of rare coins. Back in 1933, nobody really knew exactly what constituted "rare". As the decades went on, it was generally understood that any pre '33 gold coin would fit into this category. For people wanting to invest in gold, this rare coin clause was their loophole. Gold did not become legal for Americans to own in earnest until President Ford changed the rules in the mid 1970's. So, for a long time, these coins were the entire market for investing in gold (legally anyway).

Today, some investment advisors will advise staying away from pre '33 gold coins. I do not agree with them. Their argument is made based on two things: 1. Saying these coins carry a higher premium over the price of their gold metal because of their historical value. And 2. That you can be cheated more easily when dealing with these particular coins, and end up significantly overpaying for your gold coin. The reason I do not agree with these two assumptions is that with some education, and the correct frame of mind, you should not be sucked into overpaying for your gold.

These historical pre '33 gold coins also have had their reputation tarnished by people and companies pumping them as great investments. What you have are these telemarketing type companies telling people that they are rare. The fact is that as a category, they are definitely *not* rare. Individual dates and mintmarks can be very rare and sell for extremely high prices, but this is not what these unsavory companies are selling. They are selling common date coins, especially the $20 double eagle for excessively high prices. They are preying on people not being savvy investors. The second point that these types of marketing companies bring up goes something like this: "Gold bullion was confiscated in the United States back in 1933. At any time, the government may do this again, and take your bullion coins. If you buy these historic and rare coins, well...they are exempt because they're old and rare". This is just fear mongering to try to get you to hand over your hard earned money. If you hear lines like this from a seller, run the other way!

With all this in mind, you may wonder why anyone should bother with pre '33 gold coins. I can only tell you that there is nothing wrong with the coins themselves. It's only some people selling them who knowingly and purposefully misrepresent them as something they are not. There are many good, honest sellers in the marketplace. When you hold these old coins in your hand, it is amazing – you know you have something special. It's an investment in gold, but you get the added satisfaction of knowing you are holding what was considered by the public to be the epitome of "real honest money" around 100 years ago.

Here are some of my tips when buying pre '33 U.S. gold coins:

1. Stick to only $5, $10, or $20 coins. Stay away from any coin denominations under $5. You may want to even skip

the $5, and just stick with $10 and $20 coins. I include the $5 because people like lower prices especially when dipping their toes into a new type of investment. The knock against the lower denominations is that the premium over the gold price goes up the smaller the coin. The smallest of the coins carry such a high premium that you are doing yourself a disservice if you buy them. You have to think in terms of the going price per ounce that gold is trading for, and how much you are paying if you extrapolate how much you would be paying based on the size of the coin and how much gold you're getting, and for what price. While you need to allow for some markup, the lower denominations never equate to a favorable price.

2. Remember the reason you're buying this coin – to invest in gold. You should not be willing to pay more for a particular year or mintmark. These things are important to coin collecting, which is a fine hobby, but that's not the reason we're doing this. Buy common date coins that provide you a decent gold price.

3. Paying a *slight* premium for a historical pre '33 coin over a modern issue bullion coin is OK if you prefer your gold old. One way to mitigate this higher premium is to purchase a coin that has been "cleaned". Nothing destroys collecting value quite like a coin which has been cleaned, especially improperly. These coins are not desired by coin collectors, which means that they will trade in line with the price of gold and only have a very slight premium to their gold value. If you prefer the history of having old gold coins, the lower costs of a cleaned coin can be your ticket (as can scratches, dings, nicks – so long as they are not so big that you are getting less gold as a result). The upside is you get a coin that was minted to actually be used in commerce many, many years ago

4. Most of the larger gold coins ($10s and $20s) that exist are in surprisingly great shape. Even coins that dealers describe as worn, damaged, scruffy, etc. rarely look that bad to the novice. The reason is that these larger gold pieces were not routinely carried around by people. Usually, they were bank reserves – banks held them in their vaults. Wealthy people and companies had them too – in these cases they were sitting in private vaults in company offices or private home safes. The point is, they mostly didn't trade in commerce that often. These were worth a lot of purchasing power back then. If there was still a $1,000 bill printed today, do you think that you would see many people carrying it on them, or using it? I doubt it – we don't even see $100 bills that much. So it was back then. These big gold coins spent their lives in vaults of one type or another. If your intention is to buy for the gold content, stay away from pristine, mint state coins – those are collectibles.

Historic gold coins from other nations exist as well. I will say that most people living in a country prefer having coins from their own nation. Here's a tip: America is a big country and most Americans prefer U.S. gold coins. There's not much reason to pursue foreign historic gold coins, as American coins will be easier to buy and sell. Gold investors just starting out would be wise to skip the more exotic and unfamiliar issues. I will limit this section and stick to only a few of the more well known examples that are world famous:

Sovereign (Great Britain)

Weight = 7.9881 grams

Actual Gold Weight = 0.2355 OZ

Gold purity = 0.9170 or 91.70% gold)(from 1817-2001). Note minted after 2001 to present, but some special issues have a slightly different purity.

The most recognizable worldwide of the three listed. These coins feature the current king or queen of Great Britain on the front at the time they were minted. These gold sovereigns were world famous in the 19th century when the British Empire ruled a lot of the countries in the world. They are still very recognizable today due to their old British heritage. They also produced ½ sovereigns but these are nowhere near as common, so they are excluded). An interesting fact: "Even in Operation 'Desert Storm' the American pilots and the British SAS troops carried British Gold Sovereigns in their survival kits as emergency money, in case of getting shot down over Iraq."(2). It appears that in some parts of the world, a recognizable gold coin is worth more than Visa or American Express.

20 Francs Gold coins (France)

Weight = 6.4516 grams

Actual Gold Weight = 0.1867 OZ

Gold purity = 0.9000 (90% gold)

Minted 1852 – 1914. Coins have a variety of designs. The older years featured Napoleon on the front. Later coins had an angel called "standing Genius" writing the constitution. The later years featured a prominent

Rooster on the back of the coins – people still call these "Rooster coins" as a result. France also produced 5, 10, 50, and 100 Franc gold coins.

20 Francs Gold coins (Switzerland)

Weight = 6.4516 grams

Actual Gold Weight = 0.1867 OZ

Gold purity = 0.9000 (90% gold)

Minted sporadically from 1883-1949, they have the same gold content as the French 20 Francs coin. The Swiss coins have Helvetia on the front – a woman's face profile that embodies the nation of Switzerland. The back of the coins all have a variation of the Swiss cross in a shield. They also issued 10, 50, an 100 Franc gold coins.

Modern Bullion Coins

We have the modern Bullion Coins. Even though these usually carry a denomination, they were not issued to be money or used in commerce. They were minted expressly for the purpose of giving investors a product to buy as a gold investment. Here are just a few of the most popular:

American Eagle Bullion Coins

These coins are an *extremely* popular choice for American gold investors that want to own physical gold. If I had to pick just one coin for the most popular choice in America, it would be one of the coins in this series. Because they are so well known, they are very liquid, meaning you can not only buy them easily, but also sell them just as easily. Gold investors like these coins because they are easy to comprehend – the gold content of each coin corresponds to 1/10, 1/4, 1/2, or 1 ounce of gold. These coins can be confused with the historic American coins because of their similar sounding name. These are modern issue bullion coins and are generally referred to as "bullion" coins to distinguish them. They were all minted from 1986 to the present. They are designated a numerical dollar value to make them legal tender, but this is really just a symbolic gesture. The only knock against them is that usually they command a tiny premium over bullion coins from other nations due to their popularity and preference. The sizes are as follows:

Gold $5

Contains Actual gold weight = 0.1000 OZ of gold

Total weight = 3.3930 grams

Gold purity: 0.9167 (91.67% gold)

Size = 16.5mm

Gold $10

Contains Actual gold weight = 0.2500 OZ of gold

Total weight = 8.4830 grams

Gold purity: 0.9167 (91.67% gold)

Size = 22mm

Gold $25

Contains Actual gold weight = 0.5000 OZ of gold

Total weight = 16.9660 grams

Gold purity: 0.9167 (91.67% gold)

Size = 27mm

Gold $50

Contains Actual gold weight = 1.000 OZ of gold

Total weight = 33.9310grams

Gold purity: 0.9167 (91.67% gold)

Size = 32.7mm

American Buffalo gold bullion coins

The U.S. Mint added another gold coin to their product line-up. The American Buffalo gold bullion coins were authorized in 2005 and feature an old design that used to appear on U.S. nickels – an Indian head on the front and a buffalo on the back. The main difference is that these bullion coins are minted in a higher gold purity of 99.99% gold. The downside is that because of the high gold purity, the coins are more susceptible to scratching and scuffing. They are only minted in a one ounce size (4):

Gold $50

Contains Actual gold weight = 1.000 OZ of gold

Total weight = 31.108 grams

Gold purity: 0.9999 (99.99% gold)

Size = 32.70mm

South African Krugerrand

No discussion of modern gold bullion coins would be complete without talking about Krugerrands. South Africa invented the category of modern gold bullion coins when they began minting the 1 oz Krugerrand in 1967 (smaller denominations began in 1980). They get their name because Paul Kruger is on the front and a Springbok walking is on the back. Because of apartheid, the U.S. government banned the import of these coins in 1985 under President Reagan. Curiously, this ban was initiated the year before the U.S. Mint introduced their own bullion coins for sale to compete against the Krugerand. What a coincidence...you can interpret this fact however you like. The ban was lifted in 1999. These coins are not as popular as they once were, but they are still widely recognized. Denominations:

1/10 Krugerrand

Contains Actual gold weight = 0.1000 OZ of gold

Total weight = 3.3930 grams

Gold purity: 0.9170 (91.70% gold)

Size = 16.50mm

1/4 Krugerrand

Contains Actual gold weight = 0.2501 OZ of gold

Total weight = 8.4820grams

Gold purity: 0.9170 (91.70% gold)

Size = 22mm

1/2 Krugerrand

Contains Actual gold weight = 0.5001 OZ of gold

Total weight = 16.9650 grams

Gold purity: 0.9170 (91.70% gold)

Size = 27mm

Krugerrand

Contains Actual gold weight = 1.0003 OZ of gold

Total weight = 33.9300 grams

Gold purity: 0.9170 (91.70% gold)

Size = 32.7mm

Canadian Bulion Coins – "Maple Leafs"

These gold bullion coins from Canada have the queen on the front. They are commonly called "Maple Leafs" because they feature a giant maple leaf on the back. They have a higher purity of gold than most bullion coins. This is nice, but the downside is they scratch and scuff easier. Popular denominations:

$5

Contains Actual gold weight = 0.1003 OZ of gold

Total weight = 3.1200 grams

Gold purity: 0.9999 (99.99% gold)

$10

Contains Actual gold weight = 0.2503 OZ of gold

Total weight = 7.7850 grams

Gold purity: 0.9999 (99.99% gold)

$20

Contains Actual gold weight = 0.4999 OZ of gold

Total weight = 15.5515 grams

Gold purity: 0.9999 (99.99% gold)

$50 (from 1983- present)

Contains Actual gold weight = 0.9998 OZ of gold

Total weight = 31.1030 grams

Gold purity: 0.9999 (99.99% gold)

Gold Bars

They tend to be slightly cheaper than bullion coins. One reason for this is demand. Individual investors usually prefer the coins if given the choice and identical prices. One factor is that with the coins, the government minting them guarantees the amount of gold in the coin. The gold bars are produced by private companies, and these corporations guarantee the purity of their bars. Sometimes the bars are accompanied by assay cards. A corporate purity guarantee on the bars versus a government purity guarantee on the coins may explain the reason small investors usually prefer the coins. On the plus side, the bars tend to be cheaper by a small amount, and come in a much wider range of sizes compared to coins. Some of the more known companies include Pamp Suisse, Johnson Matthey, and Credit Suisse.

Exchange Traded Gold

Over the past decade or so, the idea of trading shares on a stock exchange for gold was invented. The securities trade like a stock would, except what you are buying are shares in a trust that owns gold bullion. Some of these trusts have become quite large, and may well have moved markets as they bought and sold large quantities of gold. Let's look at one of these for an example:

SPDR® Gold Shares (trading symbol GLD)

A short description from their website: (3)

"SPDR® Gold Shares (GLD) offer investors an innovative, relatively cost efficient and secure way to access the gold market. Originally listed on the New York Stock Exchange in November of 2004, and traded on NYSE Arca since December 13, 2007, SPDR® Gold Shares is the largest physically backed gold exchange traded fund (ETF) in the world. SPDR® Gold Shares also trade on the Singapore Stock Exchange, Tokyo Stock Exchange, The Stock Exchange of Hong Kong and the Mexican Stock Exchange (BMV)."

At first glance, it seems like an interesting and innovative idea. This fund certainly has become popular – their gold holdings currently stand at 710.95 Tonnes of gold. Expressed another way that's *22,857,891.18 ounces.* They report that at $1201.85 per ounce, the value of their holdings equates to a value of $27,641,792,736.17. All this information is subject to change at any moment, but I include it here as a snapshot of how big this trust is – 710 Tonnes of gold puts this private trust owning more gold than many countries.

One question everyone would be asking is where is the gold physically located? On their Frequently asked questions section, we find the answer of "Where is the gold held? Is it safe?""The gold that underlies the Trust's shares is held in the form of allocated London Good Delivery Bars, typically referred to as 400-oz bars, in the London vaults of HSBC Bank plc, the Custodian. The safekeeping methods are essentially no different from those that have operated without a problem in the London market for centuries. Those safeguards have stood the test of time for both individuals and institutions (including many governments) that store their gold in London vaults. We have confidence in the Custodian's efforts to keep the Trust's gold bullion secure. Additionally, the Custodian maintains insurance with regard to its business on such terms and conditions it considers appropriate."

A related question asks "Where is the Trust's gold physically held? "Custody of the gold bullion deposited with and held by the Trust is provided by the Custodian at its London, England vaults. The Custodian holds all of the Trust's gold in its own vault premises except when the gold has been allocated in the vault of a sub-custodian. In such cases the Custodian has agreed to use commercially reasonable efforts promptly to transport the gold from the subcustodian's vault to the Custodian's vault, at the Custodian's cost and risk. The Custodian is a market maker, clearer and approved weigher under the rules of the LBMA. More information about the subcustodians used by the Custodian is provided below..."

While the vaults of HSBC is the primary holder of the gold bars, "...The sub-custodians selected and available for use by the Custodian as of December 22, 2014 are: Bank of England, The Bank of Nova Scotia-ScotiaMocatta, Barclays Bank PLC, Deutsche Bank AG, JPMorgan Chase Bank and UBS AG."

One of the FAQs even addresses terrorism: "What happens to the gold if there is a terrorist attack and it is stolen or damaged?"

"If the Trust's gold bars are lost, damaged, stolen or destroyed under circumstances rendering a party liable to the Trust, the responsible party will be responsible. However, the responsible party may not have the financial resources sufficient to satisfy the Trust's claim. For example, as to a particular event of loss, the only source of recovery for the Trust might be limited to the Custodian, as currently it is the sole custodian holding all of the Trust's gold; or one or more subcustodians, if appointed; or, to the extent identifiable, other responsible third parties (e.g., a thief or terrorist), any or all of which may not have the financial resources (including liability insurance coverage) to satisfy a valid claim of the Trust."

You also can't exchange your shares for physical bullion. "Can an investor take physical possession of the gold backing his/her GLD shares?"

"The Trustee, The Bank of New York Mellon, does not deal directly with the public. The Trustee handles creation and redemption orders for the Trust's shares with Authorized Participants, who deal in blocks of 100,000 SPDR® Gold Shares. An individual investor wishing to exchange shares for physical gold would have to come to the appropriate arrangements with his or her broker and an Authorized Participant." This leaves us small investors out from doing this exchange.

The trust certainly makes it convenient to buy and sell gold (or "gold-backed" shares in reality) with the click of a button. I see this as its best attribute. The fact that they have arranged to hold the gold in a bank vault primarily with HSBC...I think this is both good and bad. It's good in the sense that security is probably very tight (we would hope) and thus should be better and safer than security we can provide in a house or safe deposit box at a regular neighborhood bank. Now for the potential bad side: one of the great advantages of owning physical gold in your hand is that it has value all by itself – there is no so-called "counter-party risk". This means that you are not relying on any person or institution to fulfill their end of an agreement to give value to your asset. My thought is, that the convenience you get is great, but the price you pay is that you lose one of the great reasons to own gold. The Trust does go out of their way to tell you what they have and what you own a share of – they list every single bar of gold on a spreadsheet you can download from their website. This spreadsheet lists the bar serial number and company that minted/cast it, along with total weight and gold weight. Their website makes mention that there is an audit twice a year of the physical gold.

It seems that they are going out of their way to prove to the world that everything is on the up and up. And it most probably is. But we live in a world where the news showcases people and companies that are not (think: Bernard Madoff coming to mind). I think you can make or lose money by investing in these Trust shares, depending on how much you pay and what happens to the price of gold. This is just like owning the physical gold in that regard.

But, crazy things can and do happen in real life. Even the Trust's own website has to speak of terrorism or robbery. If you're investing in gold, you most likely are looking at reducing or at least ballasting the risk from other paper assets. One can't help wondering the "What ifs". What if HSBC is robbed like in the film Ocean's

221

Eleven? What if London got annihilated in a nuclear attack (God forbid)? What if HSBC or some of its employees decided to do some kind of fraud with the gold they are watching? What if the Trust itself tried to deceive investors by issuing more shares than they have gold? What if England were invaded by another nation? (The Germans came pretty close in the early 1940's). What if____you fill in the blank. The what if questions could go on to infinity since it's limited only by your imagination of all the things that could go wrong. I think the likelihood is extremely low for any of these things actually happening. But we all know the answer to these questions – we would most likely lose all our money invested. Ultimately, it comes down to whether you think the convenience outweighs the risks or not.

Chapter 22 - Other Precious Metals

Any discussion of gold that goes on long enough eventually looks at the other precious metals that exist. While gold gets most of the glory, there are other metals that are both rare and durable. When people talk of precious metals, they are usually speaking about gold as well as the following metals. For a frame of reference, lets look at mine production of each to get a sense of rarity, at least in terms of production:

Worldwide Mine Production in Tonnes (the metric ton, equal to 1000 kilograms, or approximately 2204 pounds. The metric ton is officially called tonne):(3)(4)(5)

	2012	2013	2014	2015
Gold	2700	2800	2990	3000
Silver	25,500	26,000	26,800	27,300
Platinum	176.6	180.4	159.5	181.6
Palladium	201.7	198.2	189.9	200.6
Rhodium	22.4	21.6	19.3	22.9

Note that there are six "platinum group metals". Platinum, Palladium, and Rhodium are listed above. The three other platinum group metals – Ruthenium, Iridium, and Osmium are all very rare and mining concerns usually don't break out production figures for them. The Johnson Matthey company estimates *demand* for a couple of theses metals in tonnes as:

| Ruthenium | 19.7 | 28.0 | 27.1 | 29.0 |
| Iridium | 6.1 | 5.8 | 6.5 | 7.8 |

Note: Palladium production numbers above included Russia selling palladium stocks which amounted to 8.1 tonnes in 2012 and 3.1 tonnes in 2013, and no stock sales in 2014 and 2015.

Silver

If there was ever a metal that can be identified along with gold, it would certainly be silver. Silver was and is considered a "monetary" precious metal. Meaning, it had an official role as a circulating form of money, right along with gold. Silver has long been the running mate with gold.

Strange as it may seem, silver actually traded far more often than gold did. What? In a book about gold, how can I say this? The reason is actually pretty simple. In years past, on a day to day basis, regular folks would buy their everyday items with silver coinage. The old silver coins around today can attest to this – silver coins are often seen in a state of having heavy wear. They changed hands all the time in commerce. Gold certainly could have been used for this purpose, and it did, to a rare extent. You have to remember that at one point, a dollar was really worth a good chunk of buying power. If you got paid a dollar a day, then that silver dollar represented a whole day's worth of work. A silver dollar (or half dollar, or quarter, even a dime) had real buying power. People didn't have much need for a big, heavy gold coin to buy their basics of life. To use an analogy, suppose you went into a store today to buy a candy bar that was selling for 75 cents, and you wanted to use a $100 bill to do it. Can you do it? Yes, of course you *could*, but it would be overkill, and would most likely earn you a frown from some mom and pop cashier. So it was back in the days that gold and silver traded as money. This example is even understating it, since the $100 bill is the largest bill in print today. To make a better comparison to the way things were, consider this: the $10 gold coin and $20 gold coin were much more valuable then than a $100 bill is now. To rephrase our hypothetical situation, it would be like going into a store for that 75 cent candy bar with a $500 or $1,000 bill. Imagine the look you would get. People sometimes talk of how "back in the old days...gold was cheap..." No, it really wasn't. Even when these coins were trading at their face value, it was an extraordinary amount of purchasing power. It's likely that a lot of people in the working class never so much as ever had one of these larger gold coins in their possession.

What you had in effect was a "bimetallic" system based on both gold and silver. Gold was the high denomination coins. Silver was the "lower" denomination coins of $1 and below, which still had quite a bit of purchasing power in the old days. The real minor coins were copper pennies and nickel five cent pieces.

Gold was used as a store of wealth and reserved for large purchases. Silver was used to purchase common items on a regular shopping trip. That's why so many gold coins have survived in excellent, almost uncirculated condition. It also explains why silver coins got far heavier wear on them. Gold has gotten all the glory, but silver did the heavy lifting of keeping the wheels of commerce chugging along smoothly. This wasn't a new trend either. This had been the case long before the United States or the Americas were even known to exist to Europeans. In the ancient Roman Empire, gold and silver were both used as money. Even back then, gold was the higher denomination coin above silver.

The Silver Institute cites the World Silver Survey 2015 on the supply and demand breakdown for silver (11):

For 2014 (in Million ounces):

Mine Production 877.5

Scrap 168.5

Net Hedging Supply 15.8

TOTAL SUPPLY 1,061.8

The demand for silver for 2014 were

		% of demand
Industrial fabrication	594.9	56%
Jewelry	215.2	20.2%
Coins and Bars	196.0	18.4%
Silverware	60.7	5.7%

Note: total percentages add up to 100.3% rather than 100% due to rounding.

Coins and bars are destined for investment use by investors. Jewelry is a large share as we would expect. Silverware? While a small percent, I don't know anyone who buys or receives actual sterling silverware anymore.

I suppose even silver-plating does take some silver. We see Industry as the biggest user of silver. This is both a blessing and a curse. The demand it gives drives the price higher which is good for investors. But the flip side is that it will not help you much in a downturn in the economy, because as the economy sags, so will demand for silver, which puts downward pressure on the price. Within the industrial segment, the largest portion is Electrical and Electronics at a value of 263.9. we all know that when times get tough, electronics are among the first areas where consumers and businesses choose to cut back. Some segments are on the decline within the industrial segment, such as Photography, which now is at 45.6 and has been on the decline for years as people switch to more digital images. Other areas within Industrial have been increasing such as photovoltaic which is now at 59.9 (back in 2005, it was only at 7.3) as more solar panels are manufactured.

For an investor, you have plenty of choice with silver. Because of a much lower price, an investor can buy into silver without having to really save up much. Silver fans (ie "Silver Bugs") will frequently compare silver to gold in their explanation of why silver is undervalued. The first argument involves the historic ratio of 16:1 as the silver to gold ratio. This translates to 16 ounces of silver would be worth 1 ounce of gold. As I'm writing this, silver is trading at $14.76 an ounce while gold is trading at $1,224.60 an ounce. So we multiply 16 times $14.76 = $236.16. Some investors will say that either this means silver is extremely undervalued to gold, or gold is far overvalued. Or both. My thoughts are that an exact ratio is a little too simplistic, but the 16:1 ratio really does have precedence in history, although not always for long periods of time. With the prices that the metals are trading for today, silver is trading for a ratio of 82.96 to 1 against gold. To me, this does indeed seem very high. As to what is overvalued or undervalued, every investor must make up his or her own mind.

The second argument in favor of silver is two-fold: There are no giant silver reserves around the world as there are for gold. Thus, as hoards go, silver is more rare than gold in this respect. On top of this, mining data for silver and gold shows that worldwide silver mine production is very roughly 10 times that of gold, so this again goes back to using a ratio of silver to gold. A mine ratio would indicate a very rough 10:1 ratio. At today's prices, gold would trade at $146.60 an ounce if this ratio were applied. Again, something would be wrong with pricing. I hear that silver is underpriced by investors a lot more than gold being overpriced. Both points can be argued, so there really is no clear winner in this debate.

Some common ways to invest in silver that you should know:

<u>Historic Silver:</u>

U.S. Silver Dollars

These were minted from 1878 to 1935. The first type are called the Morgan Silver Dollar and these were minted by the U.S. from 1878 to 1904, then again for 1 year in 1921. The second type are called Peace Dollars (named after peace being achieved after World War 1). The Peace Dollars were minted from 1921 to 1935. (The Peace Dollar was actually minted again in 1964, but these were never released and were all melted down by the mint because of the withdrawal of silver from the U.S. money supply in 1965. None of the 1964 coins are known to have survived). There were silver dollars minted before 1878, but these are more rare and are priced as collectibles which is beyond the scope of this book.

Both the Morgan and Peace dollar coins are 90% silver and have 0.7734 troy ounces of silver in them. If buying them for a bullion silver investment, you'll want to buy them in "cull" condition, which means poor shape common date coins. That means they have been banged up, worn, cleaned, and heavily circulated. You do not want to pay extra for great condition or certain mintmarks. Even buying cull will mean you are going to pay more for your silver by buying the historic silver coins. These big silver coins, sometimes called "wagon wheels" are big, heavy, and old, and thus have quite a following among people. To demonstrate the price disparity, Silver is at $14.72 an ounce as I write this. So we can calculate that each of these silver dollars would have $11.38 worth of silver in them. Is this what you would expect to pay? No – a prominent online bullion dealer that adjusts its prices in real time depending on the spot price of silver were offering them at $19.75 each in cull condition. People may like these coins for their history associated with them, but you have to really pay up for this. There are much more efficient ways of investing in silver.

Modern Bullion coins

The best known to Americans are the American Silver Eagle Coins which the U.S. Mint produces. They are .999 pure silver (99.9%) and have 1 full ounce of silver in them.(they are given the symbolic $1 value denomination on them, in keeping with the tradition of the historic silver dollar coins). With the silver price at $14.72 an ounce, that same prominent online bullion dealer is offering these silver bullion coins at $18.67 each, with discounts if you buy larger quantities. So these silver coins have nearly a quarter more silver in them, and you pay *less* money. Modern bullion coins are generally a better deal than buying the old historic silver dollar coins.

The modern silver bullion coins are not limited to just the ones produced by the U.S. mint. Many nations have gotten into this act. Some of the more well known are the Canadian Silver Maple Leafs (which carry a symbolic $5 denomination on them), they are a little cheaper still...1 ounce of silver at only $17.95. The truth is that while many countries produce silver bullion coins, most Americans buy the U.S. Silver Eagle if they want an investment in silver bullion coins. There doesn't seem to be much reason to venture into buying more exotic coins than the American Eagle or Canadian Maple Leafs

Silver Bars and rounds

Silver is very popular in privately minted rounds and bars. Because of silver's relatively low price, people can often afford to buy these great big heavy bars of 10, 50, 100 ounce or larger bars. There are so many other sizes available as well. My thought is that it's like buying a low price stock. People can get carried away with the number of shares they can buy. Silver sometimes lures people with this same phenomenon. People get in this psychology of thinking that they can buy this big heavy brick of silver like you see at Fort Knox or in movies about big bank vaults (although those are big bricks made of gold). But I think the psychology is there. I'm not saying it's wrong to buy the big silver bars per se. You will get a tiny bit of money off on a per ounce basis for doing this. But remember there is a trade off. If you buy it, and the silver price goes on a tear and skyrockets in value, then you have to decide…you can either sell the big bar or hold on. With smaller bars or coins you certainly have more flexibility. You can sell a portion to realize some of the gains and keep a portion in case the price increases further. There will also be more buyers for the smaller sized coins, rounds, and smaller bars. Oh, and one more thing…you know how I mentioned that you paid a tiny bit less per ounce by buying that monster size silver brick? Well, when you do sell, you will get a tiny bit less as well. It works both ways because there isn't as much demand among people for a 100 or 1000 ounce bar. There are far more people interested in buying a smaller 1 ounce size bullion coin, round, or bar.

I would stick with buying primarily 1 ounce Bullion coins put out by the U.S. or Canada; or 1 ounce privately minted rounds or bars. I would not go above a 10 ounce bar size. I also wouldn't buy anything lower than a 1 ounce coin (except a historic silver dollar if you're really inclined by the history, and even then, I would not suggest you use them as your primary method of silver investing.). I would stay away from any smaller size because they are simply not economic. You will overpay for the silver.

Platinum Group Metals

This group includes six different elements: Platinum, Palladium, Rhodium, Ruthenium, Iridium, and Osmium.

Platinum

Of these metals, platinum is the best known. It is commonly thought to be superior to even gold. Just think – a platinum credit card is better than a gold card. For a musician, attaining a platinum status record is more of an achievement than a gold record. Platinum *usually* trades at a higher price than gold, although there are exceptions from this generality from time to time. It's been called the "rich man's gold". Like gold, it will not tarnish the way silver does. Gold is a very heavy metal, and platinum is even heavier. Platinum is "about 11% denser than gold".(12)

Part of what drives platinum to be so expensive and coveted is its rarity. Is it more rare than gold? Yes and no. If we look at scientific estimates of the rarity of platinum in earth's crust, it is about the same as gold or even a little more abundant. Using estimates that say that platinum is not even as rare as gold on earth can confuse people. While this may be theoretically true, it has one major catch. Here's the catch: platinum does not occur in the same ore density anywhere near as frequently as gold does. So while there exists gold mines scattered all across the world, platinum simply is not present in enough quantity to make mines economically viable. This is how it is. What this translates to, is that there is far less platinum dug out of the ground and refined than gold. So whether it is true or not that platinum is indeed less rare than gold, it is certainly true that it is *much more rare* out of the ground. "It takes about 10 tons of ore requiring six months of mining to produce a single ounce of platinum, according to Barisheff, who points out that platinum is 30 times rarer than gold"(1)

Platinum was in general not used as money to any great extent. Russia used platinum in some coins back in the early 1800's. Unbelievable as it may sound, at one point platinum was used to counterfeit silver coins!

Some highlights of supply and demand of Platinum(2):

In Koz ('000 ounces):

For the Year	2014	2015(est)
Total Mining Supply	5,230	5,840
Total Recycling Supply	2,040	1,890
TOTAL SUPPLY	7,270	7,730

Demand:		
Automotive	3,285	3,415
Jewelry	2,990	2,850
Industrial	1,570	1,605
Investment	150	160
TOTAL DEMAND	7,995	8,030

Balance	-725	-300
Above Ground Stocks	2,740	2,440

We can see two important things from this data:

1. Demand is exceeding supply. The amazing thing about this is that it is exceeding supply even *with* the significant contribution of recycling. The negative balance reflects the supply/demand imbalance. If we look at demand against just mining supply alone, then the demand far and away exceeds the amount produced by mining. This is usually a good sign for an investor.

2. We have to consider where the demand is coming from. The demand is coming overwhelmingly from Automotive and Industrial uses. We can lump both of these into Industrial uses. Automotive and Industrial together accounted for 62% of the demand in 2014 and 63% in 2015

What we have is a mixed bag for those looking at Platinum as a potential investment. On the positive side, it is a good sign for investors when demand is exceeding supply. This usually leads to prices increasing. The other trait platinum has going in its favor is that it is a very useful metal. It is used heavily by the automotive industry. Almost all automotive demand is for use in catalytic converters which reduces pollution. There is risk and opportunity with this fact. The opportunity comes as more and more people buy cars worldwide, and the environmental advocates push governments around the world to control pollution and greenhouse gas emissions that may be contributing to global warming. The risk is that eventually, cars may become electric powered. Then the cars wouldn't need catalytic converters in the first place. Automotive alone represented 41% of demand in 2014 and 43% of demand in 2015. That would be a big chunk of demand to potentially lose, and could severely dampen the price of platinum.

At the present time, I do not believe the world will suddenly stop using fossil fuels like gasoline and diesel to power our cars, trucks, and tractors. I think the real risk for the time being is that platinum exposes an investor to the ups and downs of the business climate. When the economy is great, the car manufacturers sell a lot more newly produced cars and this in turn drives demand for platinum. Platinum will do well when the economy does well. When there is a downturn like a recession, there is less demand for new cars and thus platinum. This lower demand knocks the price of platinum down. So platinum moves in the direction of the economy. This can be a good thing during a good market. But it does not offer the investor a safe haven the way gold does. The auto and industrial usefulness of platinum is both a blessing in good times and a curse in bad times.

One more interesting fact about platinum is where the mining production is coming from. One country – South Africa – dominates world mining production. In 2014, South Africa accounted for 59.5% of world mine production. It would have been higher, but the mining industry in South Africa went through miners striking in 2014. In 2015, South African mines accounted for an amazing 72% of world mine output. As far as reserves, South Africa has "88% of the world reserves of platinum"(12). That one country has an almost monopoly like control on platinum is incredible.

Here is the breakdown by country of mine production ('000 ounces): (13)

	2014	2015
South Africa	3,115	4,185
Russia	740	720
Zimbabwe	405	365
North America	400	385
Other	220	190

These countries are not always the most stable of places. What if a nation like South Africa ever faced worsening mining strikes? What if a more major event happened such as a civil war there? This could wreak havoc on the consumers of platinum. No doubt the price would skyrocket on these conditions. The fact that one country has such a huge share of the mining production lends a certain speculative appeal to investors.

For those looking at platinum as an investment, you will find bars and coins. The United States mint began production of platinum bullion coins in 1997. They are called Platinum Eagles and feature a prominent close-up of the Statue of Liberty on the front, and a flying eagle on the back (the proof versions meant for collectors have different scenes on the back which change every year). The United States government designated these coins official legal tender and assigned monetary values on the coins. This is symbolic, since the metal value far exceeds the face value on the coins, ensuring that people would never want to use one of these coins in commerce. Still, the 1 oz Platinum Eagle coin carries a $100 face value, so it gets the distinction of carrying the highest face value coin in the history of the United States. (the ½ oz is a $50 coin, the ¼ oz $25, and the 1/10 oz $10). While these coins come in a variety of sizes, you are better off buying either the 1 oz or ½ oz size to get more platinum for your money. The smaller denominations usually sell for unacceptably high markups from the going price of platinum.

Other countries have produced official platinum bullion coins as well. Canada mints the Platinum Maple Leaf. Australia produced platinum coins with a koala (koala coins) and a platypus (platypus coins). Austria has started production of a platinum 1 oz coin with the same design as their successful gold and silver bullion coins. The Austrian Philharmonic coins depict the Great Organ of the Golden Hall in Vienna's concert hall, the Musikverein. The reverse features an array of musical instruments. The Austrian platinum coin carries a symbolic 100 Euro denomination. Other countries that produce or have produced platinum coins include China, Isle of man, Russia, and Switzerland. There are also platinum bars of varying sizes by various refining corporations available.

Palladium

Palladium is similar to Platinum in terms of it's use for automotive catalytic converters. Palladium is even more levered to the auto industry. "...nearly 80% of world palladium supply for the manufacture of catalytic converters in cars which help reduce toxic emissions into the environment"(6). These catalytic converters use some combination of Platinum, Palladium, and Rhodium. Car makers have been able to offset a rise in price to some extent, by replacing one metal for another. If one metal spikes in price, the car maker will lessen their use of that particular metal, and use more of the other metal. They have been most successful at playing platinum and palladium against each other.

Palladium production is almost as scarce as platinum. The biggest difference is that palladium does not enjoy the same level of jewelry demand as platinum. Over the past 5 years, Platinum supply goes into jewelry to the extent that jewelry takes up anywhere from 35 to 45% of supply. For palladium, jewelry only uses between 5.5% to 8% of supply(5). Investment is not as consistent either. Johnson Matthey estimates investment as a percentage of supply ranging from 5% to 10% of supply (5) while Platinum quarterly(2) estimates investment in platinum taking up 2% of supply. Palladium has a much more irratic investment profile. In 2010, investment was around 14% of supply, but the next year, investment was a negative number, meaning net investment was below zero – the investment sector took up none of supply, but rather added supply for other demand. This happened in 2011, 2013, and 2015. At least platinum had investment demand to some degree in all these years.

Even the biggest users of palladium sometimes call it wrong. Ford Motor Company bought way too much when the price was high, and had to write off as a loss the value of their palladium holdings in 2002. "Ford Motor Co shocked Wall Street with a $1 billion write-off of the value of its stockpile of precious metals, primarily palladium. Why had the No. 2 car company made a massive bet on a commodity notorious for its price volatility?"(7). Basically they overbought, at the worst time.

For individual investors, palladium is much less mainstream as a precious metal investment. Canada minted Palladium Maple Leafs sporadically beginning in 2005. Demand was only lackluster. The United States was looking into minting a palladium eagle coin based on the design of the old Mercury dimes. "Congress authorized the Palladium Eagles under the American Eagle Palladium Bullion Coin act of 2010. Introduced in the House of Representatives only on September 22,2010, the legislation whisked through both chambers of Congress and was signed into law by President Obama on December 14th as Public Law 111-303."(8). The U.S Mint hired a company to study the issue. The findings were "it is unlikely that there will be sufficient demand for a U.S. Mint palladium bullion coin and such a program would most likely not be possible to undertake profitably. It is unlikely that there will be sufficient demand for a U.S. Mint palladium numismatic (proof or uncirculated) coin, but such a program could be undertaken profitably. 1. Pursuing such a program alone, rather than in conjunction with a bullion program, may not be in line with the U.S. Mint's usual approach to precious metals coin programs.
2. Pursuing a numismatic program without a bullion coin program additionally may not be in the purview of Public Law 111-303, which directs the U.S. Mint to focus on "the production of palladium bullion coins to provide affordable opportunities for investments in precious metals, and for other purposes."(9)

As of 2016, the U.S Mint has not produced any Palladium bullion coins. The mint obviously had pause about undertaking the program because of lack of demand. Investor beware: this should be a big red flag for anyone thinking of investing in palladium. Since the U.S. Mint paid for this study, which shows not enough demand, there may well be not much demand out there for it. If you buy palladium, it may be hard to sell it down the road when you want at a reasonable price.

Rhodium

Some get excited because the mining production of Rhodium is so small. It too, like platinum and palladium, is involved in automotive catalytic converters. In fact, catalytic converters accounts for almost all demand for this element – 83% of supply in 2015, 82% of supply in 2014. 78% of supply in 2013. 80% of supply in 2012. It has some minor uses as a finish in jewelry, mirrors, and lights. But the big use is the catalytic converters. From an investor's standpoint, that's not good. You're betting on this metal that only has one big use.

There has been interest nonetheless. It is very volatile, and I suppose there are some investors that like volatility because they want to be speculative. For example, in early 2000, rhodium was trading at about $2,000 per ounce. In early 2003, the price was down to around only $500 an ounce. In 2008, the price spiked all the way to $10,000 an ounce! Prices quickly collapsed after this. As of this writing, Rhodium is priced at about $700 (bid of $667, ask of $767- a wide spread indeed!). (10)

There will be folks who look at the price today and look back at that $10,000 price point spike and fantasize about the profit potential of a recovery. My advice is to be very careful! A lot of the world's Rhodium isn't in metal bars or coins but in powder form. I wouldn't be comfortable sinking my money into a bottle of metallic powder! One company, Baird & Company has started to refine rhodium into metal bars to satisfy investor interest. But even with these bars, it's not like when you want to sell you can just pop down to your local coin shop or jewelry store to cash in. You would be at the mercy of selling it to an online metals company that chooses to deal in these exotic metals.

The other platinum group metals – the elements Ruthenium, Iridium, and Osmium...forget them. They are rare, especially Iridium and Osmium. They are some of the world's rarest metals in terms of supply, but remember demand has to exist also. All the demand is industrial in nature. While you *can* find these elements for sale by searching the Internet, they are really sold as scientific curiosities. Some people, mostly scientists by profession, enjoy collecting different elements as a sort of intellectual hobby. This is not what we want as an investor or person looking to hedge against the decline of the dollar and other paper currencies of the world. In practical terms, if you buy this stuff, you will not get your money back. At this point, these elements are for all intents and purposes, un-investable.

I think that if you stick to gold, silver, and platinum you will have liquidity. Liquidity means how liquid your investment is – in other words how easy it is to buy and sell when you want at a price that is fair. You can buy and sell gold everywhere the world over. This is true of silver as well, and reasonably the case with platinum. When we start looking at Palladium, we are getting to the fringe of precious metal investing. Just think...All jewelry and coin shops have gold and silver. Some have platinum. All bullion companies have gold and silver, and most will have platinum. The same can't really be said for palladium. I would say that *some* bullion companies will buy and sell palladium. It's not that common because there isn't a lot of investor demand for it. For a metal like Rhodium, you're talking about really being far out there on the fringe of what's investible. There is very little liquidity. You will really have to search for a company that buys and sells this bullion. I would say stay away unless you really want to be speculative. As already stated, for metals like Ruthenium, Iridium, and Osmium, it would be wise to just forget about them – there is no market for them.

To sum it all up, Silver and Platinum are both similar and different from gold. They are both like gold in that they are widely recognized and traded commodities that can help one preserve wealth as the dollar collapses in buying power. But silver and platinum are not like gold in the sense that they will likely not protect investors in a market downturn. This is owing to the fact that both silver and platinum have massive industrial demand. While this demand by industry can be a good thing during good times, it will also be a weakness during bad times. As far as offering potential protection against a declining market and economy, gold stands alone in this regard.

Chapter 23 - Some Final Words

After reading through this book, it may seem that We The People have already lost. This is not the case.

The Fed and the international bankers that own it has America in a choke hold right now. Our nation is stumbling under the weight of the bankers running the show. It may seem impossible for us everyday citizens to battle such a mighty opponent and win. But take heart – our ancestors have faced tough fights with long odds all throughout the history of our great country. The Fed, for all its power is not invincible. In fact, it has an Achilles heel.

The Fed was brought about by an Act of Congress. For all its might, this is its weakness. Congress created it, and Congress has the power to destroy it. In fact, at any point, Congress could take a vote and abolish the Federal Reserve. Would this screw up the country? No – we would still have the U.S. Treasury to direct policy, along with the U.S. Mint to mint our coinage and the U.S. Bureau of Engraving and Printing to print paper money. In other words, the system we have would go on as before without the Fed. The biggest difference would be that We The People would not be subservient to private international banking interests controlling our money supply for their own benefit. This would be a first step toward moving to sound money again. It would open a path for gold to reclaim its traditional role as the backbone of our money supply. Throughout history, gold won against all other competitors. It was, and is, the definition of solid money. Gold will ultimately rise up again to reclaim its rightful position.

The big banks that own the Fed would be the losers. The large commercial banks would go on to live another day. But their umbrella of power over the entire United States government would be gone. They would have to operate their banking businesses just like all the other industries in our country. They would lose all the power they have in rigging the system for their benefit. This would not only be good for We The People, but may in fact turn out to be a good thing for the good banks that run their business in a sound way.

It will not be easy to accomplish this. The large banking interests that own the Fed will do anything they can to defend their grip on power. The banks contribute untold amounts of money to politicians at every level – Congress included. These politicians are indebted to them. We The People will have to remind Congress who they are really supposed to be working for in the first place. We will have to insist that they do the right thing. If they don't, then we must rise up at the grass roots level and elect new members of Congress who will.

The big international bankers may underestimate the American people. They are counting on us all to be misinformed, disillusioned, apathetic, and lazy. They are counting on us all being divided by factors such as race, gender, and religious differences and fighting each other based on these differences. They forget that We The People are used to banding together when it counts. It is in our American DNA. As Americans, we have always been the underdogs. Every red blooded American will fight for what they believe in. Our forefathers had to fight against the supremely powerful British Empire against very long odds just to become a new nation. They had to fight to keep our beloved America together during the Civil War. They had to fight the Axis powers during World

244

War 2 after the Japanese attacked our country at Pearl Harbor. And many more. In all of these cases our country won. We The People won.

If our forefathers can accomplish these victories, I think our generation of Americans is up to the task of fighting the International bankers and winning. The future is what we make of it. The future of America does not belong to the big banks. The future of America belongs to We The People.

About The Author
Dr. Louis W Piacentini

Born and raised in a suburb of Boston, Dr. Piacentini earned his Doctor of Pharmacy (PharmD) degree at the Massachusetts College of Pharmacy and Health Sciences in Boston. Dr. Piacentini is a long time bullion investor and has researched monetary policy for years. He believes in the Constitution and the liberties it bestows upon We The People. Dr. Piacentini believes in giving back to the community and was commissioned as a Captain in the Massachusetts State Defense Force. He is a member of the Ancient & Honorable Artillery Company of Massachusetts and the National Rifle Association. He is a practicing pharmacist and lives on the island of Martha's Vineyard.

You can learn more about the author on his website at:

LouisPiacentini.com

Sources

Introduction:

1. King James Bible

Chapter 1

1. Biblical Archaeology Society Staff. Why Did The Magi Bring Gold, Frankincense, and Myrrh? http://www.biblicalarchaeology.org/daily/people-cultures-in-the-bible/jesus-historical-jesus/why-did-the-magi-bring-gold-frankincense-and-myrrh/ Retrieved 3/3/2016

Chapter 2

1. Does gold Come from outer Space? BBC News Magazine By William Kremer September 19, 2013 http://www.bbc.com/news/magazine-22904141
2. World Gold Council http://www.gold.org/supply-and-demand/supply
3. http://minerals.usgs.gov/minerals/pubs/commodity/gold/mcs-2015-gold.pdf

4. http://minerals.usgs.gov/minerals/pubs/commodity/gold/mcs-2009-gold.pdf

5. http://minerals.usgs.gov/minerals/pubs/commodity/gold/mcs-2012-gold.pdf

6.http://minerals.usgs.gov/minerals/pubs/commodity/gold/gold_mcs05.pdf

7. http://minerals.usgs.gov/minerals/pubs/commodity/gold/goldmcs96.pdf
8. http://minerals.usgs.gov/minerals/pubs/commodity/gold/300399.pdf
9. http://minerals.usgs.gov/minerals/pubs/commodity/gold/300302.pdf
10. Gold Prices at onlygold.com
11. Barrick's website Barrick.com
12. http://minerals.usgs.gov/minerals/pubs/commodity/gold/300397.pdf

Chapter 3

1. http://www.gold.org/supply-and-demand/gold-demand-trends
2. http://www.morningstar.com/InvGlossary/beta.aspx
3. Annual Returns on Stock, T.Bonds and T.Bills: 1928 – Current http://pages.stern.nyu.edu/~adamodar/New_Home_Page/datafile/histretSP.html accessed 3/23/2016
4. Historical Gold Prices. Only Gold website http://onlygold.com/Info/Historical-Gold-Prices.asp accessed 3/23/2016

Chapter 4

1.Royal Canadian Mint website http://www.mint.ca/store/mint/about-the-mint/phasing-out-the-penny-6900002 retrieved 2/22/2016

2. Choron, Sandra and Harry. Money – Everything You Never Knew About Your Favorite Thing To Find, Save,

Spend, and Covet. Chronicle Books. San Francisco 2011 pg 88

Chapter 5

1 National Park Service
http://www.nps.gov/civilwar/facts.htm

2. Blackbook price guide to United States Coins. 2007

3. Gold The Race for the world's Most Seductive Metal. Matthew hartPg-50. 2013.

4. The Great inflation and Its aftermath. The past and future of American affluence. Robert J. Samuelson pg-85

5. Brown, Ellen "Revive Lincoln's Monetary Policy" Warofdebt.com retrieved July 9, 2013

6. Brands, H.W. Greenback Planet: How The Dollar Conquered The World And Threatened Civilization As We Know It. 2011 University of Texas Press pg-139

Chapter 6

1. The Fed – the Inside story of how the world's most powerful Financial Institution Drives the Markets. 2001 Martin Mayer pg-69
2. In Fed We Trust. Ben bernanke's war on the Great Panic. David Wessel 2009 pg-98-99
3. http://www.usagold.com/federalreserve.html retrieved on 01/25/2016.
4. https://www.newyorkfed.org/aboutthefed/org_nydirectors.html
5. http://money.cnn.com/2012/05/21/news/economy/jamie-dimon-new-york-fed/   accessed on 1/25/2016

6. https://www.newyorkfed.org/banks.html retrieved 1/25/2016
7. The New york federal Reserve annual reports https://www.newyorkfed.org/aboutthefed/annualreports.html
8. http://www.federalreserve.gov/faqs/about_12594.htm retrieved 1/26/2016
9. 13 bankers – The wall Street Takeover and the Next Financial Meltdown. Simon Johnson and James Kwak. 2010New York pg- 28 (quote taken from Felix salmon "Chart of the Day: Goldman VaR Reuters July 15, 2009, available at http://blogs.reuters.com/felix-salmon/2009/7/15/chart-of-the-day-goldman-var/. See also Andrew ross Sorkin "Taking a Chance on Risk, Again,"" DealBook Blog, The New York times, September 17, 2009, available at http://dealbook.blogs.nytimes.com/2009/17taking -a-chance-on-risk-again/. While VaR - value -at-risk- is a poor way of estimating potential losses under extreme market conditions, it does measure the change in the riskiness of a portfolio relative to historical data.
10. Capital – in the Twenty-First century Thomas Piketty (translated by Arthur Goldhammer) published 2014 by the President and Fellows of Harvard college Pg-548
11. Bull By The Horns. Fighting to Save Main Street From Wall Street And Wall Street From Itself. Sheila Bair 2012. Free Press New York pg-364
12. Bull By The Horns. Fighting to Save Main Street From Wall Street And Wall Street From Itself. Sheila Bair 2012. Free Press New York pg-188
13. From the website of the Chicagoo Fed file:///Users/almac/Downloads/rboc-memberbanks-19140527-pdf%20(1).pdf retrieved 1/27/2016
14. The Secrets of the Federal Reserve Eustace Mullins Evergreen Books (January 17, 2008) Chap. 3
15. The Secrets of the Federal Reserve Eustace Mullins Evergreen Books (January 17, 2008) Chap. 2
16. End the Fed. Ron Paul Grand Central publishing 2009.pg-25.

17. The Secrets of the Federal Reserve Eustace Mullins Evergreen Books (January 17, 2008) Chap. 4
18. The Alchemists. Neil Irwin. Penguin New York 2013. pg 35-36
19. The Secrets of the Federal Reserve Eustace Mullins Evergreen Books (January 17, 2008) Chap. 5
20. Mitchell-langbert.blogspot.com
21. America's Bank. The Epic Struggle to create the Federal Reserve. Roger Lowenstein Penguin Press, New York 2015 pg-85.
22. The Secrets of the Federal Reserve Eustace Mullins Evergreen Books (January 17, 2008) Chap. 5 quoted from Pawns in the Game by William Guy Carr Privately printed 1956 pg-60
23. http://www.fool.com/investing/general/2013/06/30/the-story-of-jp-morgan-the-most-powerful-bank-in-a.aspx accessed 2/2/2016
24. The House of Morgan. An American Banking Dynasty and the Rise of modern Finance. Ron Chernow Grove Press New York 2010 pg-75
25. The House of Morgan. An American Banking Dynasty and the Rise of modern Finance. Ron Chernow Grove Press New York 2010 pg-76
26. America's Bank. The Epic Struggle to create the Federal Reserve. Roger Lowenstein Penguin Press, New York 2015 Pg-71
27. Brown, Ellen Hodgson Web Of Debt – The Shocking Truth About Our Money System and How We Can break Free. Third Millennium Press. Baton Rouge, Louisiana. Fifth Edition 2012. Pg-125

Chapter 7

1. End The Fed Paul,RonGrand Central Publishing 2009 pg 90-92

2. The Courage To Act, A memoir of A Crisis and Its Aftermath. Ben S. Bernanke. W.W. Norton & Company, New York 2015 pg 33
3. The Courage To Act, A memoir of A Crisis and Its Aftermath. Ben S. Bernanke. W.W. Norton & Company, New York 2015 pg 63-64
4. Greenspan, Alan Gold and Economic Freedom Published in Ayn Rand's "Objectivist" newsletter in 1966, and reprinted in her book, *Capitalism: The Unknown Ideal*, in 1967. Accessed on 3/17/2016 on website: http://www.constitution.org/mon/greenspan_gold.htm
5. Schmid, Valentin Paul Volcker: Gold Was The Enemy. Epoch times. 3/26/2015. Accessed 3/18/2015 http://www.theepochtimes.com/n3/1299447-paul-volcker-gold-was-the-enemy/

Chapter 8

1. "Dirty 30's" www.paper-dragon.com
2. United States Department of Labor, Office of the Assistant Secretary for Administration and Management. History page, Chapter 5 Americans in Depression and War By Irving Bernstein. www.DOL.gov
3. GOLD by Mathew Hart pg-60. 2013
4. http://numismaster.com/ta/numis/Article.jsp?ad=article&ArticleId=13636

Chapter 9

1. Barisheff, Nick $10,000 Gold why Gold's Inevitable Rise Is The Investor's Safe Haven. 2013. John Wiley & Sons Canada pg-45-46.
2. Coggan,Philip Paper Promises. Debt, Money, and The New World Order. 2012. Public Affairs New York. Pg-10
3. McMorrow-Hernandez, Joshua Coin Capsule: 1974. Coinage magazine March 2016. Pg-50.
4. Coggan,Philip Paper Promises. Debt, Money, and The New World Order. 2012. Public Affairs New York. Pg-102

Chapter 10

1. Tower of Basel. The Shadowy History Of The Secret Bank that Runs The World. Adam Lebor. Public Affairs (member of Perseus Books Group). 2013. Introduction
2. BIS website https://www.bis.org/about/board.htm?m=1%7C2%7C2 retrieved 2/7/2016]
3. BIS Website https://www.bis.org/about/member_cb.htm?m=1%7C2%7C601 retrieved 2/7/2016
4. World Gold Council WORLD OFFICIAL GOLD HOLDINGS International   Financial Statistics, February 2015 (retrieved 2/7/2016)file:///Users/almac/Downloads/World_Official_Gold_Holdings_as_of_February2015_IFS%20(2).pdf
5. Tower of Basel. The Shadowy History Of The Secret Bank that Runs The World. Adam Lebor. Public Affairs (member of Perseus Books Group). 2013. Pg-265
6. Tower of Basel. The Shadowy History Of The Secret Bank that Runs The World. Adam Lebor. Public Affairs (member of Perseus Books Group). 2013. Pg-263

7. Tower of Basel. The Shadowy History Of The Secret Bank that Runs The World. Adam Lebor. Public Affairs (member of Perseus Books Group). 2013. Pg-76-77

8. Tower of Basel. The Shadowy History Of The Secret Bank that Runs The World. Adam Lebor. Public Affairs (member of Perseus Books Group). 2013. Pg-82

9. Tower of Basel. The Shadowy History Of The Secret Bank that Runs The World. Adam Lebor. Public Affairs (member of Perseus Books Group). 2013. Pg-95

10. Tower of Basel. The Shadowy History Of The Secret Bank that Runs The World. Adam Lebor. Public Affairs (member of Perseus Books Group). 2013. Pg-96

11. Tower of Basel. The Shadowy History Of The Secret Bank that Runs The World. Adam Lebor. Public Affairs (member of Perseus Books Group). 2013. Pg-114-115(from Ibid. 40.)

12. Tower of Basel. The Shadowy History Of The Secret Bank that Runs The World. Adam Lebor. Public Affairs (member of Perseus Books Group). 2013. Pg-115 (from Ibid. 40.)

13. Tower of Basel. The Shadowy History Of The Secret Bank that Runs The World. Adam Lebor. Public Affairs (member of Perseus Books Group). 2013. Pg-115 (from Cable from US Legation in Bern, June 23, 1943. NARA. RG 84, American Legation, Bern, General records. 1943: 850-851. 6, Box 92.

14. Tower of Basel. The Shadowy History Of The Secret Bank that Runs The World. Adam Lebor. Public Affairs (member of Perseus Books Group). 2013. Pg-154

15. Tower of Basel. The Shadowy History Of The Secret Bank that Runs The World. Adam Lebor. Public Affairs (member of Perseus Books Group). 2013. Pg- 133

16. The Courage to Act – A Memoir of A Crisis and Its Aftermath. Ben Bernanke WW Norton & Company. New York 2015 pg- 454

Chapter 11

1. Warren Buffett's 2011 letter to Berkshire Hathaway shareholders berkshirehathaway.com
2. CNN money article "China is dumping U.S. debt by Matt Egan September 11, 2015 money.cnn.com
3. Proverbs 22:7 Holy Bible New International version (NIV) 2011
4. Usdebtclock.org retrieved 1/25/2016
5. U.S. geological survey http://minerals.usgs.gov/minerals/pubs/commodity/gold/mcs-2015-gold.pdf
6. http://www.forbes.com/sites/afontevecchia/2011/07/13/bernanke-fights-ron-paul-in-congress-golds-not-money/2/#5688b3916486
7. World Gold Council file:///Users/almac/Downloads/World_Official_Gold_Holdings_as_of_February2015_IFS.pdf

Chapter 12

1. Value Line Investment Survey for Bank of America. August 14, 2015 by Theresa Brophy
2. Value Line Investment Survey for Tootsie Roll Industries. October 23, 2015 by Michael Lavery
3. Taken from Value line Aug.15 2015 issue on the Bank Industry reports

Chapter 13

1. Williamson, Kevin D. Accursed Wall Street – Our ritual, shallow denunciations of the finance industry. National Review magazine March. 14, 2016 Pg 16.
2. ValueLine Investment Survey

3.   Scheer, Robert The Great American Stickup. Nation Books New York. 2010 pg – 234-235

4.   Thoma, Mark Clinton on Glass-Steagall: Right or Wrong? November 16 2015 http://www.cbsnews.com/news/clinton-on-glass-steagall-right-or-wrong/ accessed 3/15/2016

5.   Scheer, Robert The Great American Stickup. Nation Books New York. 2010 pg – 54-55

6.   Beaty, Johnathan and Gwynne, S.C. with Cathy Booth/Miami- Jay Branegan/Hong Kong and Helen Gibson?London Monday July 29, 1991 from TIME Website. http://www.bibliotecapleyades.net/sociopolitica/sociopol_globalbanking118.htm accessed 3/15/2016

7.   Lohr, Steve World-Class Fraud: How B.C.C.I. Pulled It Off -- A special report.; At the End of a Twisted Trail, Piggy Bank for a Favored Few The New York Times 8/12/1991 http://www.nytimes.com/1991/08/12/business/world-class-fraud-bcci-pulled-it-off-special-report-end-twisted-trail-piggy-bank.html?pagewanted=all accessed 3/15/2016

Chapter 14

1. The rise and Fall of the Third Reich. A History of Nazi Germany. William L. Shirer. 1959, 1990pg- 51
2. The rise and Fall of the Third Reich. A History of Nazi Germany. William L. Shirer. 1959, 1990pg- 58
3. The rise and Fall of the Third Reich. A History of Nazi Germany. William L. Shirer. 1959, 1990pg- 62

4. Hitlerland. American Eyewitnesses to the Nazi Rise to power 2012 Andrew NagorskiPg-42
5. Hitlerland. American Eyewitnesses to the Nazi Rise to power 2012 Andrew NagorskiPg-41-42
6. The rise and Fall of the Third Reich. A History of Nazi Germany. William L. Shirer. 1959, 1990pg- 61
7. Nationalww2museum,org By the numbers: World – Wide deaths

Chapter 15

1. The Death of money . the coming collapse of the international monetary system. pg-220. By Jamecs Rickards 2014.
2. called "Gold – the Race for the World's most seductive metal by Matthew Hart 2013.
3. $10,000 Gold. Why Gold's Inevitable Rise Is the Investor's Safe Haven. Pg-6 by Nick Barissheff 2013
4. Bernanke Fights Ron Paul in Congress: Gold Isn't Money. Forbes http://www.forbes.com/sites/afontevecchia/2011/07/13/bernanke-fights-ron-paul-in-congress-golds-not-money/#2715e4857a0b6a0e047c48db

Chapter 17

1. Harper, Jennifer The Washington Times. May 11 2015 http://www.washingtontimes.com/news/2015/may/11/liberal-speakers-dominate-college-commencement-six/ accessed 3/14/2016
2. Legal Information Institute. Cornell University Law School https://www.law.cornell.edu/wex/second_amendment accessed 3/14/2016

3. Starnes, Todd Student punished for saying "bless you" Fox News 8/20/2014 http://www.foxnews.com/opinion/2014/08/20/student-punished-for-saying-bless.html accessed 3/14,2016
4. Herzog, Ashley Atheists Lose Battle To Remove "In God We Trust" From U.S. Currency The Political Insider. http://www.thepoliticalinsider.com/atheists-lose-battle/ accessed 3/14/2016

Chapter 18

1. Employer's gold, silver payroll standard may bring hard time. Las Vegas Review-Journal may 29, 2009 http://www.reviewjournal.com/news/employers-gold-silver-payroll-standard-may-bring-hard-time (retrieved 2/8/2016

2. Use Real money, go to federal prison Bryan Hyde March 26

   2012

   http://www.stgeorgeutah.com/news/archive/2012/03/26/use-real-

   money-go-to-federal-prison/#.Vrl-0bkrKL0 (retrieved 2/8/2016)

3. The Fascinating Reason a Wi. Restaurant Gives Huge Discounts to Customers Who pay With Coins Minted Before 1965 June 28, 2013 http://www.theblaze.com/stories/2013/06/28/the-fascinating-reason-why-a-wis-restaurant-gives-huge-

discounts-to-customers-who-pay-with-coins-minted-before-1965/ (retrived 2/8/2016)

4. Newcomb, Rosette Your Turn Hillary- Sanders Reveals What his Paid Speeches Look Like Feb 19 2016. Retrieved 3/5/2016 http://usuncut.com/politics/bernie-calls-out-hillary-releases-transcripts-paid-speeches/

5. Griffin, G. Edward The Creature from Jekyll Island. A Second Look at the Federal Reserve. Fourth Edition American Media, Westlake Village, California, 2002. Pg-325-326.

6. Griffin, G. Edward The Creature from Jekyll Island. A Second Look at the Federal Reserve. Fourth Edition American Media, Westlake Village, California, 2002. Pg-327. Quoting Rothbard, *Mystery*, pp 194-95

7. Griffin, G. Edward The Creature from Jekyll Island. A Second Look at the Federal Reserve. Fourth Edition American Media, Westlake Village, California, 2002. Pg-330.

8. Griffin, G. Edward The Creature from Jekyll Island. A Second Look at the Federal Reserve. Fourth Edition American Media, Westlake Village, California, 2002. Pg-331 Quote from Galbraith p. 72

9. Griffin, G. Edward The Creature from Jekyll Island. A Second Look at the Federal Reserve. Fourth Edition American Media, Westlake Village, California, 2002. Pg-331 Quoted Derek Wilson P. 178

10. Griffin, G. Edward The Creature from Jekyll Island. A Second Look at the Federal Reserve. Fourth Edition American Media, Westlake Village, California, 2002. Pg-331 Gustavus Myers, History of the Great American Fortunes. New York: Random House, 1936, p. 556.

11. Griffin, G. Edward The Creature from Jekyll Island. A Second Look at the Federal Reserve. Fourth Edition American Media, Westlake Village, California, 2002. Pg-331

12. Griffin, G. Edward The Creature from Jekyll Island. A Second Look at the Federal Reserve. Fourth Edition American Media, Westlake Village, California, 2002. Pg-336

13. Griffin, G. Edward The Creature from Jekyll Island. A Second Look at the Federal Reserve. Fourth Edition American Media, Westlake Village, California, 2002. Pg-342-343

14. Griffin, G. Edward The Creature from Jekyll Island. A Second Look at the Federal Reserve. Fourth Edition American Media, Westlake Village, California, 2002. Pg-357

15. Brown, Ellen Hodgson. The Web of Debt. The shocking Truth About Our Money System and How We Can Break Free. Fifth Edition 2012. Third Millenium Press, Baton Rouge, Louisiana Pg-75

16. Mullins, Eustace The Secrets of the Federal Reserve. Chap. 5

17. Harwick, Cameron "Crytocurrency and the Problem of Intermediation . The Independent Review Volume 20 Number 4 Spring 2016.

Chapter 19

1. Ancient Greek Economics being Proved In Modern Greece: Gresham's Law. Tim Worstall Forbes. July 4, 2015 accessed 2/12/2016 http://www.forbes.com/sites/timworstall/2015/07/0 4/ancient-greek-economics-being-proved-in-modern-greece-greshams-law/#153d124c3dc1

Chapter 21

1. Standard Catalog of World Gold Coins 6th Edition. Krause Publications. Lola, WI, 2009.
2. 10 Things You Should Know About The British Gold Sovereign. August 20, 2011 by Dom. Accessed 2/15/2016 http://www.mastersoftrivia.com/blog/2011/08/10-things-you-should-know-about-the-british-gold-sovereign/

3. http://www.spdrgoldshares.com/ accessed 2/16/2016
4. U.S. Mint Website
   https://www.usmint.gov/mint_programs/buffalo24k/?action=amBuffBull
   Accessed 4/7/2016

Chapter 22

1. Saefong, Myra P. Platinum's a precious metal, too" MarketWatch July 29, 2011.
   http://www.marketwatch.com/story/platinums-a-precious-metal-too-2011-07-29 Retrieved 2/25/2016.
2. Platinum Quarterly Q3 2015
   https://www.platinuminvestment.com/files/WPIC_Platinum_Quarterly_Q3_2015.pdf retrieved 2/27/2016
3. US Geological Survey reports
   http://minerals.usgs.gov/minerals/pubs/commodity/gold/mcs-2016-gold.pdf
   http://minerals.usgs.gov/minerals/pubs/commodity/gold/mcs-2015-gold.pdf
   http://minerals.usgs.gov/minerals/pubs/commodity/gold/mcs-2014-gold.pdf
4. U.S. Geological Survey on Silver
   http://minerals.usgs.gov/minerals/pubs/commodity/silver/mcs-2014-silve.pdf
   http://minerals.usgs.gov/minerals/pubs/commodity/silver/mcs-2015-silve.pdf
   http://minerals.usgs.gov/minerals/pubs/commodity/silver/mcs-2016-silve.pdf

5. PGM Market Report November 2015 by Johnson Matthey Precious Metals
   http://www.platinum.matthey.com/documents/new-item/pgm%20market%20reports/pgm%20market%20report%20november%202015.pdf accessed 4/8/2016

6. North American Palladium Ltd. http://www.napalladium.com/palladium/supply-and-demand/default.aspx Retrieved 2/28/2016.

7. White, Gregory L. A mismanaged Palladium Stockpile was Catalyst for Ford's Write-Off. 2/2/2016Wall street Journal accessed 2/28/2016 http://www.wsj.com/articles/SB10129447173368862 40

8. Accessed 2/28/2016 http://palladiumeagles.us/

9. U.S. Mint website accessed 2/28/2016. http://www.usmint.gov/about_the_mint/?action=palla diumreport

10. Metal price of Rhodium from Kitco http://www.kitco.com/charts/rhodium.html accessed 2/28/2016

11. The Silver Institute website https://www.silverinstitute.org/site/supply-demand/ accessed 2/28/2016 the source:The Silver Survey 2015

12. Vronsky, I.M. Platinum: The Rich Man's Gold. May 1, 1997. http://www.gold-eagle.com/article/platinum-rich-mans-gold retrieved 3/1/2016

13. World Platinum Investment Council. Platinum Quarterly Q3 2015. November 24 2015. https://www.platinuminvestment.com/files/WPIC_Pla tinum_Quarterly_Q3_2015.pdf Accessed 4/8/2016

www.ingramcontent.com/pod-product-compliance
Lightning Source LLC
Chambersburg PA
CBHW021421170526
45164CB00001B/47